Praise for Our Fear Never Sleeps

"Wow. Fantastic. This is a powerful deeply personal story relatable to anyone, introducing tools to be comfortable with the uncomfortable. The value of being vulnerable in front of peers, family and friends teaching us lessons about trust, choice and being present and intentional. The story brings these tools to life to learn to let go, breakthrough and move forward towards what you say you care about most."

Steve Byrnes, Chief Sales Officer, Ascentis

"Our Fear Never Sleeps is a true hero's journey every single one of us can use as a guidebook for our own. Imagine where the world would be if we each found the courage and wisdom to choose clarity over certainty and to let our lizard brain rest so our hearts can lead the way. Erik and Moira's sharing of their personal and shared journey is incredibly powerful and full of insight that we can all put into action immediately."

Kirsten Gunnerud, Founder, Rocket Trike

"When my dad first told me about you writing a story about your son's journey, my first thought was everyone has hardships, why is this one special? But after reading it, I learned so much more about myself than I have in years. In just about every chapter I learned something new. All I can say is thank you for lending me a copy."

College Student

"I have worked with Erik for ten years, his mentorship and applied learning tools have changed me as a business leader and as a husband, father, and friend. Being self-aware and completely present while approaching conversations with positive intention is game changing. Thank you, Erik and Moira, for sharing your story with me, life happens, you show us how we can overcome anything by letting go to fight for what IS possible."

Kevin Newman, President, Electric Power Generation – Americas, a Nidec Company

"When a book challenges your mind or creates a gut reaction it is a compelling one that we seek to read. When a book challenges your life, your beliefs, and your attitude, potentially for good, then it is something different: it is a singular opportunity for real and sustainable growth, that can't be missed. This story does all of that. Therefore, I call it a blessing!

Moira and Erik crafted a real gift in these pages. It is the promise of unleashing unimaginable potential, even when the odds might not look favorable. They give hope, a way, and tools to make them real."

Dr. Gaia Marchisio, Executive Director, Cox Family Enterprise Center, Kennesaw State University

"As a parent I found this book compelling at every turn of the page. As a pediatrician, I recognized that any physician caring for children could benefit from reading this honest and raw story of hope and doubt from parents who found themselves in a situation with so much uncertainty. We can never fully understand the powerful backstories of all the beautiful children for whom we provide care. Through their experiences, Erik and Moira provide a framework and checkpoints helpful for any parent trying to be the best person they can be while creating an environment in which their child can thrive."

Paul Melchert, MD, Pediatric Hospitalist

*Lessons From Our Son's Survival
And What It Took To Save Him*

Our Fear
Never Sleeps

Let Go To Fight For What's Possible

Erik Gabrielson and Moira Petit

INDIE BOOKS
INTERNATIONAL

ISBN: 978-1-947480-86-5
Library of Congress Control Number: 2019918488

Designed by Joni McPherson, mcphersongraphics.com

Cover and illustrations by Timothy Foss, morebelief.com

INDIE BOOKS INTERNATIONAL, INC.
2424 VISTA WAY, SUITE 316
OCEANSIDE, CA 92054

www.indiebooksintl.com

For Kieran, who taught us to love, live, and experience joy with exuberance.

We couldn't imagine a world you didn't touch. You are our biggest gift.

Table of Contents

Authors' Note ix

Prologue xi

Part One – Waking Up 1

   1 – Life Happens While Making Other Plans 3

   2 – The Fight To Survive 19

Photos I 37

Part Two - Surviving to Thriving 41

   3 – Expand Your Comfort Zone 43

   4 – The Power Of Choice 59

   5 – Adjust Your Filter 69

   6 – The Stories We Tell 87

   7 – Strive For Clarity 101

   8 – The Ordinary Moments 115

   9 – The Myth Of The Aha! 127

   10 – Create A Powerful Learning Community 139

Part Three – Lessons From Kieran 151

   11 – Grateful 153

   12 – Let Me Show You My Scars 159

Photos II 163

Acknowledgements 169

About The Authors 173

Works Referenced 175

Authors' Note

Erik and Moira: Our Test

In 2007, our unborn son was diagnosed with a likely fatal birth defect. We would both be deeply challenged by the experience and forced to examine our tightly held beliefs about who we were individually and as a family.

We found ourselves way beyond our comfort zone. Until then we had been able to compartmentalize the perceived separate areas of our lives. The unknown future of our son brought a high level of awareness that our work and personal life were not separate, but rather tightly integrated and influencing one another.

Our son's journey became our own test of the collective body of work we coach in the arena of human potential. This story is about the intersection of our journey with our son and the work we've had the fortune of doing since 2002 (Erik) and jointly since 2010.

As a couple, we each responded differently to our son's diagnosis and the experience we shared. For Erik, it was about the fight for what was possible, and for Moira, it was about letting go. Eventually, we found the intersection that allowed us to collaborate. We would both need to *let go to fight for what's possible.*

This story is about what it took for us to navigate the unknown as our personal and professional lives collided. Often, a distinction is made between the two. We pretend to be different people in different areas of our lives, when actually the two are merged, all aspects of life impacting the other. We see in our work how separating them can limit what is possible in each area of our lives.

In part one we share our personal story and the uncertainty about our son's survival. In part two we incorporate some of the concepts from our work as human potential coaches that came alive for us during our journey. We also share stories from clients and the hospital team that reflect a broad application of these principles. Some names have been changed to protect the privacy of those depicted.

In our work, we often facilitate experiences that get people outside of their comfort zone and serve as a mirror for how they show up in life. Our son became that mirror for us. He challenged us to see our experiences from a new perspective and consider how we were showing up in the world. He revealed the potential and resiliency of being human, to experience what is possible when people choose to be part of something bigger than themselves.

Our son's diagnosis magnified our fears as parents. We realized that fear would drive our behavior if we let it. Fear would get in the way of our son surviving and thriving. The fear was always there. We had to find a way to navigate it and continue to take action—to learn. We would need to apply the principles we coach to our own lives.

We don't pretend to have the answers for you, the reader. This is the story of our personal exploration of our experience and the principles that helped us lead our lives within an often-chaotic journey.

We hope sharing our journey creates more questions for you than answers, and inspires you to explore yours.

Prologue

Erik: A Good Question

I woke up in a mist. The sun was a faint glow through the fog. The morning dew dampened my sleeping bag while the crisp chill invited me to stay in it a little longer. I woke up thinking, "Why am I paying for a retreat where my options for sleeping are a Dojo's grapple mat with fifteen other guys, or outside under the stars with no tent?"

I chose the stars. The risk of getting wet was more appetizing to me than trying to sleep with fifteen other guys snoring next to me.

It was the first day of a six-day leadership program at the Strozzi Institute, put on by two human performance coaches who had just finished six months leading the *Marine Warrior Project*. They were now introducing the concepts and principles into the civilian population. A friend of mine had convinced me that I should attend. I was resistant and skeptical, thinking it would be rah-rah crap that I wanted nothing to do with.

As it turned out, I was incredibly fortunate to be part of this beta program. The coaches had a deep competency in human potential and a strong history of supporting high performance in individuals, athletic teams, the military, and in organizations all over the world. The same principles and experiences they applied in military settings were also critical for optimizing human potential regardless of the circumstances. It would end up being a life-changing week for me.

After waking up in a bed of wet long grass, I hung my sleeping bag in a tree to dry off. I made my way into the common area and the kitchen to help make breakfast. Larry Burback, one of the leaders of the program, had captured the attention of the people in the room. He was giving everyone an update on the Tour de France from the previous day. As a leader of the program, he had the luxury of sleeping inside and watching the race the night before.

Larry had a confidence, calmness, and intention about him that demanded attention. As he spoke it was apparent that he was passionate about life. I would later learn that his motto was: "I refuse to tiptoe through life to safely arrive at death." At the time, he was in his mid-fifties, about six feet tall with an athletic sinewy frame. He had a Freddie Mercury mustache and a bald head. His intensity was palpable and screamed, "Don't screw with me," while having an openness and curiosity that drew me in.

I connected with Larry immediately. Sleeping outside for the week, I had no access to a TV or the internet and was totally unplugged. Larry was my conduit to the Tour de France. Our bike conversations led us to explore the many similar passions we had for life. Our friendship began, as well as his mentorship.

Larry was curious and asked questions. He learned I ski raced growing up, coached skiing and applied those skills into business. He challenged my assessments of the world. At the time, I was struggling with the path I was on in both my work and personal life. I felt stuck and fearful of the uncertainty of making a big change.

A few days into the week Larry asked, "Do you want something to be better in your life?"

I looked at him hesitantly and said, "Yes."

He responded, "Okay, so that means you want to learn something?"

"Yes," I said again.

"Great, when we talk about learning we define it as the ability to take a new and different action than you were able to before." Larry explained. "Knowledge and content are just the beginning. It becomes learning when you apply that knowledge toward what you care about. The mind understands and the body learns. Learning happens through experience, through taking action."

Larry continued: "This is not rocket science. You did it growing up ski racing, and you coached other skiers to do the same. You know how to take action within fear. My question to you is, why are you not doing it in your life where the consequences are much greater?"

Good question, I thought. Larry continued, "I see many people who get clear on commitments, develop practices and work through fear in athletics and hobbies. Few actually do that same thing in their life. As a result, they put their fulfillment and joy at risk."

It was the right question at the right time. Little did I know just how big the consequences would become. At the time, I didn't realize how much Larry's mentorship and the human performance framework would impact my ability to step into the life I desired. I didn't realize just how difficult that would be.

It wasn't until several years later when I had started collaborating with Larry and was expecting my first child that Larry's question would really sink in. It became apparent that I had much to learn. I would need to take very different actions than I had in the past.

Part One
Waking Up

1

Life Happens While Making Other Plans

Erik: The Diagnosis

My wife, Moira, and I thought it was just a routine mid-term pregnancy ultrasound. So far everything with the pregnancy had gone smoothly. We thought our biggest concern going into the ultrasound was whether or not we should find out the sex of our baby. Luckily, both of us agreed, we wanted it to be a surprise.

A vacation had pushed back our appointment a couple of weeks to December 26. As a result, Moira was over twenty weeks pregnant, the typical time to have a mid-term ultrasound.

We arrived at the appointment with great hope and excitement for the future.

We left with a recommendation from the doctor to end the pregnancy.

The lyrics of the 1980 song "Beautiful Boy," written by John Lennon for his son Sean, contain the famous line, "Life is what happens while you're busy making other plans." That hard truth became suddenly apparent to us.

Little did we know that death would be part of our child's life even before he was born.

A few days before the ultrasound appointment we had just arrived back home from two weeks in Mexico with Moira's family in time to spend Christmas with my family. The trip to Mexico was an annual tradition, an escape from the holiday mayhem. I enjoyed arriving back home just as the pace of others was slowing down to enjoy the holidays.

This year was a little different than past years since Moira was pregnant with our first child. As we were lounging on the beaches of Isla Mujeres, Moira and I had extra time to think and talk about our new life as parents. We were excited, and as prospective parents, had no idea what was in front of us.

We made a commitment to each other that our lifestyle was not going to change much. We were still going to travel, and I was convinced I would continue skiing in the mountains as much as I wanted. Life was going to be great. It is only one kid we thought. We have the energy to do all of this.

As we walked into our ultrasound appointment, I was reflecting on how fortunate I was as my excitement about the future was growing. We arrived at the office waiting room and checked in. The technician soon led us into the exam room and explained the process as Moira laid down on the exam table.

The technician rubbed gel all over Moira's stomach and asked, "How are you feeling? Any concerns I should know about?"

Moira responded with a smile, "None that I know of."

Moira tilted her head back and to the side so she could see the screen. The technician pointed out, "There is your baby's head and its feet. You can see the hands and heartbeat."

It was so amazing to see our baby clearly on the screen; it looked all good to me. The technician kept moving the ultrasound probe. Then stopped abruptly. She pressed some buttons to take some still pictures, studied the screen, and looked over at us with concern on her face.

"See this? This doesn't look right," the technician said. She continued to move the probe and kept quiet.

Thirty seconds or so went by and I asked her, "What did you mean, that doesn't look right?"

She replied, "Your baby's stomach is not in the right place. Just wait here." And she left the room.

Moira was on the bed with goop all over her. She and I sat there looking at each other not knowing what to say. I could feel my breath getting shallower, my jaw clinching telling myself, "Just take a deep breath." Then thinking: "What is she doing? Where did she go? What in the hell is that all about?"

The picture of our baby was still on the monitor. We kept alternating our focus from each other to the monitor trying to understand what was going on. "What did the tech mean?" I wondered.

Leaning closer to Moira, I squeezed her hand.

Ten or fifteen minutes went by. It could have been a minute or an hour; it felt like a day. The technician finally walked back into the room with our prenatal doctor. The doctor pulled the monitor closer and pointed to an area that she said was the baby's chest.

"I'm sorry to tell you that your baby has a severe form of Congenital Diaphragmatic Hernia (CDH)," said the doctor.

Moira and I looked at each other, squeezed our hands harder together and looked back. We had no idea what she was talking about. We had never heard of CDH.

The doctor filled in some medical details that we didn't fully comprehend at the time and then said, "Given my calculations, your baby has a severe form of CDH and I do not expect this child to survive."

The doctor went on to explain that if our child did survive, it would likely not be more than a short time and its quality of life would be extremely poor.

Given Moira was already over twenty weeks pregnant and additional genetic testing would take a few weeks, our doctor said, "I strongly recommend that you terminate this pregnancy now."

I moved as close to Moira as I could. Shocked, we looked at each other, not knowing how to respond. I really did not want to believe what the doctor was saying. How can she tell all that just from looking at a picture? It was too soon to be sad. I was mad. Disbelief took over.

The doctor printed off screen shots of our baby then wiped the gel off Moira. She wanted to have a follow up appointment in a week to discuss where we go from here.

After that, I don't remember much. The world shut down around me. I couldn't hear, I couldn't feel, I was sick to my stomach. We perfunctorily thanked the doctor and left the building.

We walked out of the clinic and Moira turned to me, hugged me and said, "What are we going to do?"

"I don't know," was all I could say.

Moira: Meeting Erik

I was thirty-six when I "finally" (according to my mother) got married, and thirty-seven when I became pregnant. My pregnancy was considered a geriatric pregnancy, the clinical term they used at the time for a pregnancy that occurs when a woman is over thirty-five. So, I knew there may be increased risks with my pregnancy.

Being married and having children was never a specific aspiration of mine. I enjoyed having the freedom to explore the world, engage in trail running and other outdoor experiences, and pursue a career that I felt was meaningful.

When Erik and I met, I had just moved back to the Twin Cities (Minneapolis/St. Paul, Minnesota) after a decade away. I had spent the previous decade doing academic work in British Columbia and Pennsylvania. I had just landed a tenure-track faculty position at the University of Minnesota and had negotiated what I felt was a great start-up package that would set me up to be successful in my research and teaching. I was enjoying work, running and reconnecting with family and friends. My life felt full and I would have been happy to keep that focus.

Then I met Erik. When we first met, I wasn't quite sure what to make of him. Erik was intense and excited about everything he did. He saw possibilities everywhere he turned and put his full energy into whatever came his way.

At first, I thought he was crazy. No one could possibly be this energetic and excited about life, I thought. My skeptical nature made me think he must be inauthentic. This must be some salesy thing he learned through his real estate background and leadership work. I certainly didn't want to trust a business guy from Edina, Minnesota.

As I got to know him, it was clear that there was nothing inauthentic about him. He was as real as it gets. Erik openly shared his history and struggles with his work and his past relationships. It was clear from the way he talked about his experiences that he knew he didn't have everything figured out, and he was curious and open to learning.

Still, I had some strong assessments about Erik's career choices as a real estate developer and human potential coach and what that must say about him. Eventually I couldn't deny that I loved how I felt being around Erik and my biggest concern was that he was too excited about life. Clearly that said more about me than him.

When we became engaged, my age precipitated the constant question of "When are you going to have children?" I personally did not feel pressure to quickly get pregnant after our wedding, or at all. Erik and I both had independent lives and many of our own interests; we would be happy without children. I was not completely opposed to having children, either. If it happens, that would be cool, if it doesn't, so be it.

At my age, I knew the challenges of getting pregnant and was aware of the increased risk of conditions like Down syndrome, among others. I had watched friends go through their own challenges with fertility. I had great respect for the couples who were so committed to parenthood that they worked with fertility experts, experiencing an emotional and physical roller coaster of in vitro fertilization (IVF) and other treatments. Yet, I was equally sure that route was not for me.

Given that, I was wonderfully surprised when I realized I was pregnant just a short time after we pulled the goalie (as we say in hockey country). It took me about ten positive pregnancy tests to fully believe it was true, and before I even mentioned it to Erik.

My first reaction to the pregnancy was to be cautiously optimistic, knowing the risks, particularly in the first trimester. I am Scots-Irish, after all. We can't get too excited about anything or something bad will happen (think potato famine).

I was prepared for the very real possibility of a miscarriage as I'd seen friends experience early on. I tried to put those thoughts aside and just enjoy, but not get overly excited about the early part of my pregnancy.

As the bump in my belly grew and my body changed, there was no denying there was a real child in there. I started to enjoy the feeling of pregnancy. I let myself smile at the idea of impending parenthood. It felt good. It felt exciting to think about parenting with Erik. He was so full of optimism and energy it balanced and centered me. We would have *fun*.

Then came the diagnosis. Not Down syndrome, not a miscarriage, not anything related to my advanced maternal age or our genetic history. The diagnosis of CDH was something I'd never heard of. With all that my friends had endured in their own fertility journeys, none had this kind of a diagnosis.

Terminating a pregnancy was a somewhat abstract idea to me. It was something that rumors were whispered about *that poor girl* in high school and college. Intellectually, from a social-cultural perspective, I firmly believed women should have that choice. In practice, I was fortunate not to have to make that kind of choice back then.

Now, I wasn't a twenty-something who didn't have the resources or support to carry and care for a child. I was thirty-seven with an established career, loving husband, and supportive family. Erik and I had willingly, and with full awareness of the consequences, chosen to engage in an act that would result in creating a new life. Now I was more than twenty weeks pregnant with a child growing inside me.

There was urgency to make a decision because I was already more than twenty weeks pregnant. The additional information that would give us more insight would not be available soon enough for us to legally end the pregnancy.

I felt fortunate to have the option for a safe and effective procedure if that was the route we chose. This was a significant and critical diagnosis. It would be life changing and no matter the outcome, our child would endure significant pain and struggle.

And yet, how could we possibly make this choice?

Erik: Meeting Moira

"I'll do my best," Moira promised to me as we wed in 2006. She explained to me, "How can I say 'I do' when I have no idea what is in front of us? At this time all I can really promise is that I am here and I will do my best, which is 100 percent, but I can't predict the future."

When we were married we loved each other, yet we still did not know each other (or even ourselves fully). We had not gone through a significant struggle together. The diagnosis of our unborn baby was a tornado that came out of nowhere and changed that. We had no warning, no preparation, and no knowledge of what it was. It felt like a freight train coming right at us so loud I could not hear any other noise. Everything was wiped away except for the two of us standing looking around asking ourselves, "What do we do now?"

Our history would help inform our next actions.

Moira and I met in a triathlon-training group in the Twin Cities and, as it turned out, we had gone to the same college one year apart. We soon discovered that we had similar connections and were at many of the same parties in college.

Moira was independent, strong, demanding, caring, generous, and a fireball. She was confident in the life she was pursuing. It did not take long for me to see that I wanted more than a casual relationship. I don't think she was quite as smitten with me as I was with her.

The more we spent time together, the more our time became adventures. We found ourselves traveling and exploring together. We would go on running and biking trips and the experiences became more meaningful because I was doing them with Moira.

I thought that maybe she was starting to feel a deeper connection to me when she picked me up at my house and drove to the airport without telling me where we were going. She surprised me by planning a weekend in Chicago to see the band U2 at the United Center. I was falling for her adventurous spirit and willingness to engage in life.

After a couple years of dating, I decided to ask her father, Pat, out for coffee to get his blessing on our marriage. When I called him to ask him to meet, he was a little resistant to getting together, wondering what my motivation was. After some convincing he decided he would make the time.

About twenty minutes into our coffee I looked at Pat and said, "The reason I wanted to have coffee was because I want to ask your daughter to marry me." He laughed and immediately responded, "You don't want to do that Erik, not an independent woman like that. You know what that will be like? Do you know why those Scottish women are so independent?" He went on, "Because back in the day their husbands would go out to war and their heads would come back separated from their bodies. The women had to do it all on their own. Those Scottish ones are strong, you know."

I couldn't believe what I was hearing. What was his angle? Then he started to go on about how wonderful Moira was and how he was so proud of her. "She is the best of the lot, isn't she?" he stated. Pat continued his dialogue about how proud he was, and it became clear that he was protective of his daughter. He wanted to make sure I knew how lucky I was.

Moira: Research Mode

The day after the diagnosis I went into research mode. At the time, I was a faculty member at the University of Minnesota, advising a number of graduate students.

Within twenty-four hours we had gathered every published paper on CDH we could find. I had a stack of research papers explaining what CDH is, why it happens (they don't know), clinical outcomes, and the hospitals in the world that specialize in it.

Erik likes to say I became obsessive. Maybe I was. The academic in me was convinced there would be something in the data that would help inform our decision. I looked through all the published manuscripts and spent my time on the computer researching the data, the issues, possible procedures and hospitals. I was arming us with information.

The more we read, the more overwhelmed we became.

Babies with severe CDH like our son's have consistently low survival rates. When the diaphragm does not fully form during development, organs migrate up into the chest cavity. This reduces the space in the chest cavity for the lungs to form properly. In our son's case, his stomach, a portion of his intestines and a part of the liver had all moved up into the chest cavity. He indeed had a severe form of CDH and according to the data, had a less than 25 percent chance of surviving.

In addition to reduced space for the lungs to form, our child's heart was pushed out of place, increasing the possibility of heart damage. Our son also had a very low lung area to head circumference ratio (LHR), another indicator, used at the time, of a low chance of survival and poor prognosis.

Given the severity of our child's condition, the data were not good. As we reviewed the literature, the future that was being painted for our child was disheartening. Even if our child did survive, he would likely have a bleak future according to the data.

One review article[1] published the year after Kieran was born summed up what I was reading about the journey ahead of us. It stated things like: "…life threatening anomaly…many complications including pulmonary damage, cardiovascular disease, intestinal disease, neurocognitive defects, musculoskeletal abnormalities and failure to thrive…more long-term consequences…GERD, high incidence of esophagitis, Barrett's esophagus, and oral aversion…" If our child were to be put on extracorporeal membrane oxygenation (ECMO, a high-risk treatment that does the work of the lungs and heart and a likely procedure in our child's case), there was a high incidence of neurological deficits and becoming deaf.

We had to consider the reality of the evidence.

Moira: Letting Go

Shortly after our ultrasound appointment we were at a movie, *U2 3D*, escaping the stress of the diagnosis as we enjoyed Bono's voice and Edge's riffs. During one of our favorite U2 songs, I looked over at Erik, grabbed his hand and put it on my stomach. "Feel this," I said. "He is kicking to the beat of the song."

When I felt our baby kick, that was it for me. There was a real live child growing and thriving inside of me. After that, the choice for me wasn't about terminating the pregnancy or not. This was a live person inside me that I could feel moving, that I was deeply connected to. For me, we had already committed to the journey and this child was part of us now. There was no turning back.

---

[1] MG Peetsold, et al. "The long-term follow-up of patients with a congenital diaphragmatic hernia: a broad spectrum of morbidity." *Pediatric Surgery International* 25 (2009):1-17.

Fortunately, Erik agreed. We were both all in. From that moment, it became not about the choice of whether to have the baby, but about our next choice. How were we going to show up?

Yet I couldn't shake the academic in me that understood the reality of the clinical data. I thought if I looked hard enough, I would find something that would tell me what to do to improve our child's outcomes. Some pill I could take, some exercise I could do or not do, some specialist I could see.

That's not what I was reading though. If I focused on the quantitative data, it made no sense to continue the pregnancy. The future for our child was so bleak. At a minimum, he would require significant medical intervention and resources. At the same time, he felt so strong as he moved and kicked in my stomach.

A wise family friend said, "All you can do is love him as he is right now." That thought centered and grounded me. Literally all I could do was to be present with him in this moment. The time he was in my stomach might be all I had with him.

For me, I had to find a way to let go. Let go of the data and any ideas I had about what our child's, or our, future would look like. Let go of wanting to do something or know what was coming. Literally the only thing I could do was just be.

Once I was able to do that, all the unimportant stuff fell away. I started to realize how many things I spent energy worrying about that I really had no influence over. Letting go became something I would need to practice over and over. When I was able to, it allowed me to actually enjoy my pregnancy even with all the uncertainty.

Erik: The Gift

Before the diagnosis I was somewhat detached from the pregnancy. There was something growing inside my wife's stomach and it was going to show up in a few months. I was sure our child would not change our world too much. We would just integrate him into our active lifestyle and bring him along on the ride, literally and figuratively.

The diagnosis changed my perspective. I suddenly realized that I couldn't wait until he was born to have a relationship with him. For all I knew the only relationship I might have with my son was while he was in Moira's stomach. I shifted from detachment to having a strong desire to be connected and in a relationship with him starting right now.

"One way to do that is give him a name," Moira said.

"Yeah, that's a great idea," I responded. I had affectionately been calling our baby "It." As, "Is it kicking?" "What is it doing now?"

As we thought back and did the math, we realized he was conceived while we were in Colorado earlier that year participating in the Pikes Peak Ascent and Marathon. Both Moira and I had passions for the outdoors and participating in various athletic endeavors. We had really enjoyed all the time we spent together training for, and participating in, the events together.

"What about Pike?" I said to Moira. She laughed at first, though immediately liked it, too. Pike felt good and it made us smile. It felt strong and like he was a part of us and our journey together. Our only hesitation is that living in Minnesota we realized people might think we were referring to a fish. We got over that, and it felt good to give him the temporary name of Pike.

Once we named our baby, something shifted in me. I started to have conversations with him, asking him questions, asking Moira questions about him and wondering out loud what he was thinking. I enjoyed talking to him, rather than at him. I started to imagine his personality and began to be in a relationship with Pike.

My relationship with our son helped me realize that every moment going forward was a gift. A gift to me, a gift to Moira, a gift to our relationship. Our child's diagnosis and our commitment to him changed how we saw the world around us. I realized nothing was a given. Each moment became an experience to be savored. I felt joy rather than dread.

For me, the diagnosis became about a fight. A fight for what was possible. A fight for our child's future. I wanted him to determine that future. I reached a place of accepting what the current state was and shifting my energy to fighting for what could be.

This fight was not only about the child growing inside Moira. It was also about our future, our life together.

Erik: Searching For A Future

Both of us fought the urge to find certainty. We realized certainty didn't exist for us anymore. This experience would teach us that it never did. There was no certain path that we could see to having a healthy baby. This diagnosis created an awareness for me that I didn't have before. The more data we collected, the less certain we were.

The data were not telling us what to do. We craved just a bit of information that told us it would be okay (or at least the possibility of it being okay). That wasn't what we were reading or hearing. We had to get to a place where we could accept that it probably wouldn't be.

As we struggled with the uncertainty we struggled with our decision. Our conversations and energy went from trying to forecast what the future might be, to simply being on the journey and showing up the best we could. The quantitative data we were reviewing was now being informed by our emotions, desires and experiences, creating context for our decision-making.

Up until then there was a collective story that was being told, by the data and the doctors, about what was possible for our child. Moira was astute enough to realize that the biggest thing in the way of our child's future would be our own fears. This realization allowed us to change our point of view and start to focus on how to support our child in determining his own future, rather than the collective determining it for him.

To get there, Moira reached a place where she was able to let go of the future she envisioned, along with all the data that was getting in the way for her. I reached a place of accepting what was, and fighting for our child's future, whatever that may be. It would take our joint perspectives to come together and collaborate for our family's future. We had to let go, in order to fight for what might be possible.

This was an important shift for us. It allowed us to create a filter for our decision-making. We were able to make one decision at a time, and not focus on the overwhelm and what would never be. We could now focus on the next step that would give our child a possibility to create a future. The clarity of focusing on supporting his possibility allowed us to navigate the uncertainty. It allowed us to acknowledge our fears and then take action anyhow.

2

The Fight To Survive

Moira: The Hospital Search

Armed with my research, I went to the follow-up appointment with the obstetrician. I ended up seeing a partner of the doctor who made the initial diagnosis.

This doctor had a similar narrative and agreed there was little chance for our baby to survive. He quoted an outcome study published in the early 1970s that showed children with the severity of our son's diagnosis had no (as in zero) chance of survival.

I was a bit surprised that the doctor was quoting data from so long ago. I knew that technology and treatment protocols had changed significantly even in the last few years. I also understood enough about the timeline of clinical research to know that the published data were not always reflective of current clinical practice. I was hoping to hear about the doctor's experience in practice.

It was clear from the data I had seen that even in the last few years there had been significant strides in how babies with CDH were treated. As a result, their probability of survival and quality of life were increasing, although the survival and outcome data were still very poor for children with a diagnosis as severe as our child's.

As with most conditions, outcomes for babies with CDH were improved with increased clinical experience so I asked the doctor, "How many babies with CDH do you care for each year?"

"Usually no more than one or two, but we have a great Neonatal Intensive Care Unit (NICU)," he said.

That sealed it. This was not the right place for us. I left there committed to finding a new hospital.

Our search for the right place was not a confidence-building process. We explored options from going to Germany to have in-utero fetal surgery, to hospitals on the east and west coast where they had extensive experience treating babies who had CDH.

We heard generally some version of the same story. "We agree that your baby has a severe form of CDH and has a less than 25 percent chance of survival and will face many complications. We will do what we can."

Erik had a strong reaction to the prognosis we were getting. He recalls "I wanted to scream at them and ask them what the hell did that mean? What happens to those 25 percent who do survive? What causes the 75 percent to die? What can you do for *our* child?"

My reaction was more tempered. I knew this was an impossible situation for all of us and the doctors couldn't make any promises. I knew we, and they, were entering the unknown. At this point, I was just tired. The thought of moving to a different city or doing something extreme like going to Germany for an in-utero surgery felt exhausting.

I was fully committed to supporting our baby and giving him the best possible chance. But how far did that mean we should go? Would it really require we leave our jobs, friends and families and move to another city or country for an unknown amount of time and for an unknown outcome?

During a night out for dinner, we shared our story with a physician friend who suggested we check out the local children's hospital. For some reason it wasn't even on our radar. Our friend, who we highly respected, said, "Their neonatal intensive care unit has a great reputation and from what I've seen, they have a great approach for babies with CDH."

When we met with the team at the local children's hospital, we immediately knew it was the right place for us. After taking the time to give us a full tour of their NICU unit and introduce us to their team, the head neonatologist said something like "We agree that based only on the data in front of us, your baby has a low chance of survival. However, those data only predict the average. They do not tell us what is going to happen to your baby. Our commitment is to each individual family and child. We assume that each child can and will survive and thrive until they don't. Each life is an individual fight."

After a worldwide search, we ended up a few miles from where we lived, at the Minneapolis campus of Children's Minnesota. It was only a fifteen-minute drive to the hospital from our house. We didn't yet realize just how fortunate we were to have landed with this team.

Moira: Settling In

From the outside, we looked like any other happy couple expecting a baby. Inside though, the fears were constantly present. My mind quickly and easily wandered to the fact that the ever-growing child inside me might not survive. I saw everything through that filter and the fear would quickly set in. I panicked at gas stations thinking the fumes would cause more harm to my baby's lungs, or if I hadn't eaten in a while I would irrationally think I had to get food in me *right now!* or Pike might not survive.

At some point the continued practice of letting go helped me be present and involved in life—even enjoying it. I think I pulled it off most of the time, though there were some challenges. When people asked if they could throw us a baby shower for example, I would reply something like, "No thank you. I don't know if my child will survive or need newborn gifts. Thank you, though."

I was put on bed rest in late March about six weeks before the baby's due date. I started having contractions and it was critical that Pike not come early. Each week closer to his due date meant a significant increase in his chance of survival, so I needed to keep him growing as long as possible.

Somehow Erik and I both really enjoyed those weeks. We would binge watch Netflix shows, marveling at each time our baby kicked or moved. There was a kind of acceptance and peace that there was nothing more we could do right now other than just be there with Pike.

Erik: Birth

The day had arrived: May 5, 2008. Our son was being born.

We arrived at the hospital at 7:00 a.m. to have Moira induced. We scheduled the birth to ensure the team of specialists was there and ready to help save our son's life.

Our family was gathered in the waiting room for support and by 9:00 p.m. it was clear this kid wasn't going to come out on his own. Moira had spent the day patiently waiting, sometimes in great pain, for our baby to come and he had managed to get his head stuck. He was already showing us that he was not going to make anything easy. The doctor ordered an immediate C-section.

Earlier in the day a surgeon from the NICU team visited our room to request I sign releases that gave all decision-making rights to the care providers. The doctor shared, "There will be critical moments when we will need to make decisions for your son in order to save his life. We won't have time to ask your permission in those moments."

The biggest decision would probably be whether to put our baby on extracorporeal membrane oxygenation (ECMO), a highly risky method of oxygenating the blood outside of the body.

The doctor stated, "The risks of ECMO are substantial. One of the biggest risks will be internal bleeding that can cause a stroke in the brain. When babies are on ECMO they need to be on high doses of blood thinner so that the blood can run through the machine, be oxygenated and pumped back into the body." The doctor mentioned a number of other highly risky aspects to the procedure that I didn't fully comprehend.

"Do you understand these risks?" the doctor asked me. "Sure," I said with hesitation. Never having been through this before, I heard the words but really had no idea what they meant. We had chosen this team to take care of our child and had put our trust in them. It was out of our hands; it would be up to Pike and the NICU team.

Just before 10:00 p.m. the nurse returned with a gown, slippers and surgical cap for me to put on. We went into the pre-op room, washed up and made sure I was ready to enter the operating room.

Moira was lying on the table groggy with her stomach cut wide open. The nurses all were intently listening to the doctor and supporting the surgery. There was a feeling of urgency and focus. I sat next to Moira's head with a line of sight to what the doctor was doing. I held Moira's hand tight and just talked to her. "Everything is going well; our baby is just about here."

In an adjacent room, a team of five people were ready and waiting to help our son fight for his life. After cutting the umbilical cord, he would not be able to breath on his own. Without significant medical intervention he would only have a few minutes of life before he died.

One of the nurses stepped through the door into the operating room, ready to receive our son.

Once he was out of Moira's womb, our baby never stopped moving. As the doctor pulled him out, someone cut his umbilical cord as the delivery doctor handed him to the nurse in waiting. He was in the next room intubated instantly so he could get enough oxygen to breathe. It felt frantic and, to me, chaotic.

A nurse opened the door and said to me, "Could you please come with us, we need a parent to join us on our journey to the NICU." I stood up and hesitated for a moment. They were asking me to leave my wife on the operating table, and my son was waiting.

I let go of Moira's hand and left her lying on the table with her stomach still cut open. She never had a chance to see her baby. I walked through the door and looked at our son, laying in the incubator, desperately wanting to hold him.

I glanced back at Moira through the window as the team whisked Pike away toward the NICU. All I could do was run alongside and watch.

None of what I imagined the birth of my child to be was happening. A tube was put down my newborn child's throat to help him breathe, so he never had a chance to cry. He was in an enclosed incubator that was on the move, so I couldn't hold or touch him. My wife was now in a different building and had yet to see her son.

As we entered the NICU, the doctor approached me and said, "Thank you for coming, we've got it. There is nothing more you can do here right now. Why don't you go back to Mom?"

I stayed for a minute or so. Confused and exhausted I stood and watched the constant activity. I felt helpless. My son had a team of people poking him, shoving needles in him; helping him breathe, and they asked me to step out of the room. I still hadn't touched him. I hadn't been able to look into his eyes.

I eventually found Moira in a recovery area. She was lying on a gurney in pain, groggy and puffed up. They had been pumping her full of fluids and drugs all day and she looked like she was about to explode. How must she feel right now? Beyond exhausted, delirious, and having just given birth but not yet able to see her son. I felt useless—what could I do to comfort her? I sat next to her and was still for a bit.

"I asked, "How are you doing?"

"I don't know", she said, then asked, "Where is our son?"

"He is in the NICU and stabilized for now. They told me to leave and come back here," I replied.

The doctors told us to wait a bit before I brought Moira over to see our baby. The two of us were silent. It was almost too much to think. At any moment we could be notified that Pike didn't make it. We really didn't know what he was going through and what the NICU team was doing to keep him alive.

Moira: A Glimpse

At first, I didn't want Pike to be born. He was safe and he was *alive* inside my stomach. He wouldn't be able to breathe on his own as soon as he came out and he might not live for more than a few seconds.

After fifteen hours of labor, various drugs and fluids being pumped into me, I was exhausted. By the time they decided to do a C-section, I was more than ready to get that kid out. I simply couldn't keep him safe anymore.

On the table I was partially awake but not feeling anything as Erik sat next to me and our baby came out surrounded by the clinical team. The rest of the evening was a blur until I woke up in a recovery area that felt like a utility closet. It was dark and it seemed that no one else was around. I had no idea what was happening with our child—was he even alive? At some point Erik walked in and moved me to another room. It felt surreal, like we were in our own little world.

Back in our room we got a call from the NICU that we could come and visit our son. My first thought was that I just wanted to stay where I was and sleep—I could see him later after I rested. Then I remembered he might not live and if I didn't go now, I may never see him alive. I quickly thought, "That would be tragic if you never saw your son alive. You'd better figure out how to get down there, now!"

I couldn't sit up yet from my surgery, so I was lying on the gurney that Erik had to steer down a long tunnel over to the NICU. We didn't even reach the elevator before I started throwing up. It seemed to come in a constant stream after that. I kept blaming Erik's driving for my nausea, though he claims that had nothing to do with it.

Erik pushed me through the NICU to the back where our son was. He had a tube sticking out of his mouth: his ventilator, that was breathing for him. Other tubes were hooked up to him along with multiple wires, dispensing drugs and gathering information. The team was working furiously around him. All I could do was turn my head one way and glance over. All the machines were blocking my sight and I could barely get a glimpse of the top of his head. I didn't have the energy to lift my head anymore—I just wanted to throw up and feel better. I vomited again. We were there for less than five minutes and were told to go back to our room and let the team do their work.

Erik: Uncertain Future

Soon after we made it back to our room, we received a call from Pike's doctor. She said, "Your son is stable at this time. I just wanted to let you know. I will try to report in intermittently to keep you updated of his status."

This allowed us time to focus on each other for a while. I could focus on Moira and just sit for a moment. Our son was born. He was alive for now, and he was in a building across the street from us.

A couple hours later, we heard the phone ring. I answered and mumbled something. The voice on the line said, "Is this Erik?"

"Ahh, yes, it is," I responded.

"This is your son's doctor from the NICU. I wanted to let you know that your son is not doing well. We were convinced he would die without some help, so we just finished doing surgery and hooked him up to the ECMO machine. He seems to be stabilized for the moment and we have a team monitoring him. We need to make sure he gets fully stabilized before you come over to see him. It is about 3:00 a.m. now. Why don't you come over around 6:00 a.m.?"

"Ahh. Okay. Thanks." I replied. "We are doing everything we can, and I anticipate that he will stabilize over the next couple of hours. See you in the morning," she said, as I heard the click of the line disconnect.

Moira was looking at me, listening to the phone call. I couldn't keep from crying and crawled into bed with Moira. We both just lay there, silent and motionless.

I awoke early and made a quick coffee run, arriving back about 5:45 a.m. Moira and I made eye contact as I entered the room. We didn't need words to communicate what we were both thinking…is our son alive? We had not received any more calls, so we assumed that he was. It was time to go visit him.

As I wheeled Moira into the NICU, she became focused on the baby back in the corner whose designated area was larger than any of the others. It seemed as though Pike had a whole wing of the NICU to himself with the many machines needed to keep him alive.

I couldn't see where our baby was among all the equipment until we were right next to his bed. He was motionless, eyes closed and lying on his side. In his mouth was a ventilator breathing for him. Two big tubes (cannulae) were in the right side of his neck.

Pike was motionless because of the paralytics that were flowing through his body. One of the tubes that connected our son to the ECMO machine went through a jugular vein to drain blood from his heart; the other pumped the blood back into a carotid artery. Pike's right lung was just a tiny sliver and his left lung could not be seen at this point—much too small to work on their own—so the ECMO machine bypassed his lungs and did the work of oxygenating the blood for him and helped his heart pump it to all his vital organs. He could not afford to move because if those tubes were to become unattached, he would die instantly.

So, he just lay still on the bed, motionless. I was wondering what level of awareness to the world he had. Could he think? Could he feel his blood flowing through his body? I wonder if he senses that things aren't right, I wonder if he knows he is alive?

Pike required two full-time nurses by his side 24/7. They were monitoring his condition, testing and adjusting the machines and drugs as needed. All I could hear was the ventilator breathing for him. Hiss in and hiss out. Hiss in and hiss out. His chest would rise and fall with the sounds of the machine. His blood was being pumped out of his body and back in. The nurses were making minute-by-minute adjustments. It was overwhelming.

"Good morning. I'm Heidi, your son's nurse. He is stable and doing okay. He has had quite a night." "Good morning," we said back as we just stared at the baby in front of us. "Go ahead and hold his hand," Heidi said as she gestured toward our son. We touched him for the first time. No response.

We both continued to hold his hand, trying to comprehend what was happening. I felt powerless. How could we connect and take it all in?

As Moira and I sat next to Pike in the NICU, it was apparent that the only influence we had on our son's life was our will and the positive energy we directed toward him. It did not feel as though we were his parents. It felt like we were observers as the nurses and doctors kept him alive. We had yet to look into his eyes. They remained shut, as he lay motionless. We had not yet held him. We had no control over any part of his life. All we could do was watch the commotion, talk to each other and talk to our son even if he was unable to respond.

Standing and sitting next to his bed would be our foreseeable future. It created a space for me to think about him and how we got to this place where he had a chance. A chance to fight. This journey continued to be a gift to me and my relationship with Moira.

It allowed me to become focused on what was important in my life, giving me the opportunity to connect to our son, Moira and me. My son was already teaching me about my life through his.

Erik: I'm Here

The early days flew by. Nothing seemed to change much: the nurses were monitoring Pike, adjusting drug doses and drip rates on numerous machines as needed, the various monitors attached to Pike beeping and beeping while he lay motionless.

It was a place of contrasts. There was heavy activity with a sense of calm; life in danger and the optimism was palpable; people with acute focus were executing, saving lives, yet you could see smiles and hear laughter; one family hearing tough news while another was rejoicing. We didn't have to look far to see others with bigger challenges in front of them. It was a place of survival at its best. It was a place to fight for your life.

My mind just kept filling up with the thoughts of our journey so far. How did we get here? I heard somebody once say, "When you are in a place of scrambling for what you want, the days feel long and the time goes fast." That feeling was appropriate to me at that moment. It felt as if we were just at the ultrasound appointment when we received the diagnosis. Yet, each day felt exhausting. So much had transpired, and we still had so far to go.

Sometime around his third day, as Moira was watching him, she said, "I saw his toe move," and she instantly started to cry. It was beautiful. It was the first time she saw her baby move. It was the first signal from him saying, "I'm here; I am alive."

Moira: A Name to Live For

We were resistant to giving Pike a permanent name at first. As hopeful as we were, we knew there was always the possibility he wouldn't survive more than a few days.

The nurses kept reminding us that they needed a permanent name. "What should we call your baby?" they would ask. "We want to call him by his name and we need a legal one in the hospital."

Around the third day, after we saw his toe move, we decided we were ready to give him a real name.

We agreed on Kieran, a name I had always loved. I'd always fondly remembered an adorable family friend named Kieran I'd met in Scotland when I was young. It connected to my heritage and since Erik got the last name, I figured I could choose the first name. Fortunately, Erik liked the name and quickly agreed. We also added two middle names, Patrick Petit, my father's name. Kieran Patrick Petit Gabrielson. It felt long, but strong and right. Connected to all his people. This kid would need all the connection he could get.

On the fourth day after Kieran's birth, I had my staples removed and was recovered enough to leave the hospital. We decided to make a quick trip home.

As we were walking in the skyway to the parking garage Erik and I both felt sick to our stomachs. It was so hard to leave Kieran. The feeling of nausea and dread was overwhelming. What if we don't get to see him again?

It was the reality of our life at the moment. Our baby could die at any moment and if we left, we might not be there with him when it happened. Just another reminder of how little control we had and of the fears we would need to navigate.

Erik: The Surgery

We showed up at the hospital early in the morning on May 15th. Kieran was ten days old. This was a big day. Today was the day that could save our child's life.

Kieran had little to no diaphragm on his left side. His stomach, intestines, and a portion of his liver had floated up into his chest cavity because the diaphragm was not there to serve as a barrier keeping the organs in their proper place. This had pushed his heart over to the side and did not leave room for his lungs to develop properly.

During surgery, Kieran's doctors would move the organs in his chest back down into his abdomen and then put in a prosthetic diaphragm. All of this would be happening while he was still on ECMO having the machine continue to do the work of his heart and lungs. If successful, the hope was that the small amount of lung tissue he had would expand once space was made available and he would eventually start to breathe on his own.

We washed and foamed our hands and stood next to Kieran's bed. We asked his nurse how he was doing, and she said, "He had a really good night. The surgery is scheduled for today."

She was already prepping him and organizing his bed. The NICU was on the third floor and the surgery center was on the second floor. Kieran would need to be transported, with all his machines still hooked up, into the elevator and down to the second floor in order to have the surgery.

The preparations took all morning and now it was time to move him. It took four people to move him, all his machines, and oversee that nothing went wrong during the move. The ECMO machine was particularly sensitive. If anything went wrong during the move, he could get a brain bleed or other damage. The move itself took over an hour to get him down one floor to the surgery center. They moved him an inch at a time.

We walked down with Kieran and watched them wheel him into the operating room.

As we watched him go in, we were hopeful that we would see him come out. The hospital had a visual system that kept us up to date on what stage the surgery was in. A digital chart on the wall that showed whether he was in prep or surgery or recovery. I tried to keep my thoughts positive, and that was hard over the many hours that we waited. My mind wanted to wander to all the what-ifs.

About four hours later, the digital chart told us that the surgery was complete, and Kieran was in the recovery room. His surgeon came to get us and brought us to a private room. He held up an x-ray picture and explained what was going on with Kieran and what he did. First, Kieran was alive! It was a successful surgery, although harder and longer than expected.

The surgeon explained how challenging surgery can be with little babies in general, due to their small size. In Kieran's case, the left side of his diaphragm was essentially nonexistent so there was not much to attach the diaphragm-like patch to. It was made of a new biological tissue with the hope it would grow with him and meld with scar tissue.

Kieran was still intubated, not breathing on his own and still on ECMO. He was doing okay coming out of anesthesia and would be in recovery for a while. A big first step.

We found a somewhat private place in the hallway and cried. Neither one of us could control our emotions. We were so happy and relieved and elated and exhausted all at the same time.

When Kieran was recovered enough to head back to the NICU, it again took four people and over an hour to get him and his equipment back up one floor. Despite the successful surgery, he would still need to be attached to the risky ECMO machine to give his lungs time to develop more. We were hardly out of the woods yet.

We settled into a routine in the hospital of visiting Kieran, monitoring his ups and downs and trying to understand all the complex medical information that was being thrown at us. Our days were a mix of uncertainty, relief, dread, and moments of gratitude and joy.

One night, we were sleeping at home and received a call in the middle of the night. We were always on high alert for the phone ringing, so I grabbed it quickly. The doctor said, "I wanted to let you know that your son is struggling and not very stable." I was confused as he was doing great when we left him earlier that evening.

"What is wrong with him?" I asked as I was holding my breath and my hand was shaking.

"He is struggling and is unstable. We don't know if he'll make it through the night. I suggest you come to the hospital immediately."

We of course rushed out the door and spent one of many tense nights at the hospital hoping Kieran would make it through. We would experience several more nights and days like this in the months to come.

Moira: A New Filter

I've read that the first thing a newborn does is assess their environment for safety. Apart from physical needs for air, food, and shelter, an infant's primary need is to feel safe and connected. The first days and weeks are critical for developing a sense of comfort and security.

Rather than comfort and security, Kieran's early experience was filled with discomfort, trauma, and isolation. In his first twenty-four hours of life, our son had a breathing tube put down his throat, underwent surgery, and would be placed on enough paralytics to put down a large horse. In his first few months of life, Kieran would spend fourteen days on ECMO, he would be intubated and extubated several times, have several surgeries, experience multiple ups and downs and close calls. He would not breathe without assistance and he would only receive his food through a tube initially placed through his nose, and later directly into his small intestine bypassing both his mouth and stomach. The invoice for his first four weeks of life was over one million dollars, much of that in pharmacy costs alone.

We couldn't hold Kieran for several weeks because of all his equipment. All we could do was sit there and sometimes we were able to touch his hand or forehead. His nurse was brilliant. When he would scream in pain (early on with no sound because of the breathing tube, and later with an intense gut-wrenching scream), she would rub his forehead and say "That's it. Tell me all about it. Tell me everything." She would just be present with him and let him work through it in his own time.

I would remember that for many years to come when Kieran continued to struggle with pain and intense emotions. My temptation was always to step in and solve it for him as if I could somehow force him to feel better. That never worked, of course. Instead, I would remember Heidi and would just hold him and rub his forehead and say, "Tell me all about it." Another level of letting go for me.

Moira: Coming Home

Gradually, Kieran would gain some strength and start to smile. We were able to hold him (within the confines of his bed and under the close watch of his nurses so we didn't disturb any of his tubes), read him stories, and see him start to interact and connect with us. He achieved many large hurdles such as coming off the ECMO machine, breathing with *just* a ventilator, and eventually with just an oxygen cannula.

After nine weeks of many struggles, near death moments and heart-wrenching withdrawal symptoms, Kieran was moved out of the NICU to the Infant Care Center (ICC), a unit for babies who were still sick though in a less critical condition. We were so excited when we were told he was strong enough to leave the NICU. Still, we were told, he would likely need another month or more of hospital time. That's OK, we thought. We can wait. This is huge progress.

One evening, just two days after Kieran was moved to the ICC, we were sitting next to his bed watching him smile and interact. One of his doctors came in the room and said "We've decided that Kieran can go home tomorrow. You'll need to take some classes in the morning to learn CPR and how to manage his feeding tube and oxygen tank, but you can take him home in the afternoon."

Wait, *what?*

"Oh shit," we thought, "we have a lot of work to do tonight." We still had not prepared anything at home since we didn't want to jinx him. No crib or baby room, no clothes or diapers. Plus—CPR, feeding tube, oxygen tank. What? We were filled with a mix of elation, fear, and joy all at once.

Kieran came home nine weeks after his birth on July 3. We celebrated by hanging out in our backyard with our dog, Kieran, and all his gear. We opened a bottle of champagne. We were thrilled.

Little did we know—our learning was just beginning.

PHOTOS I

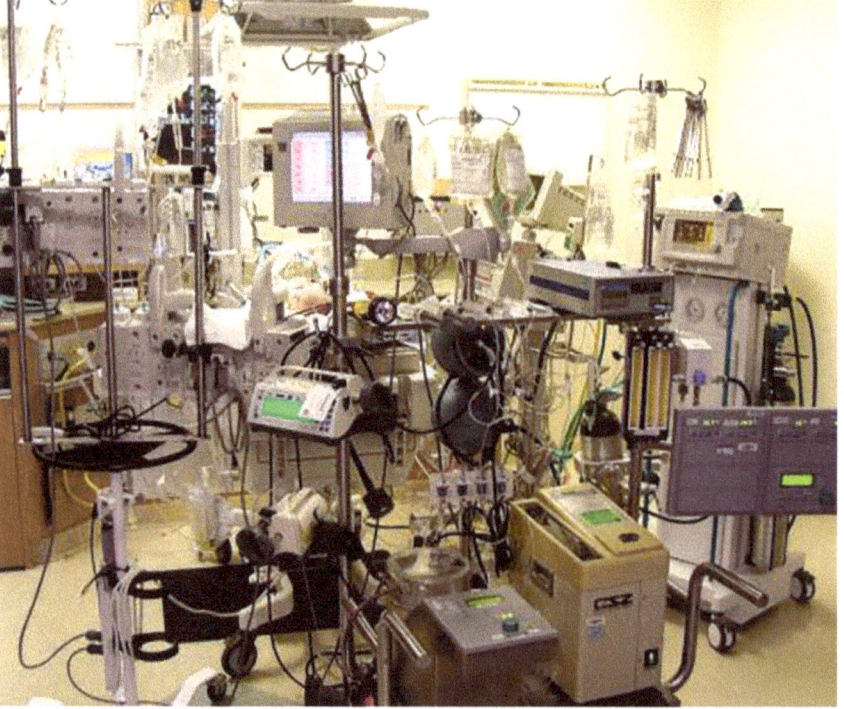

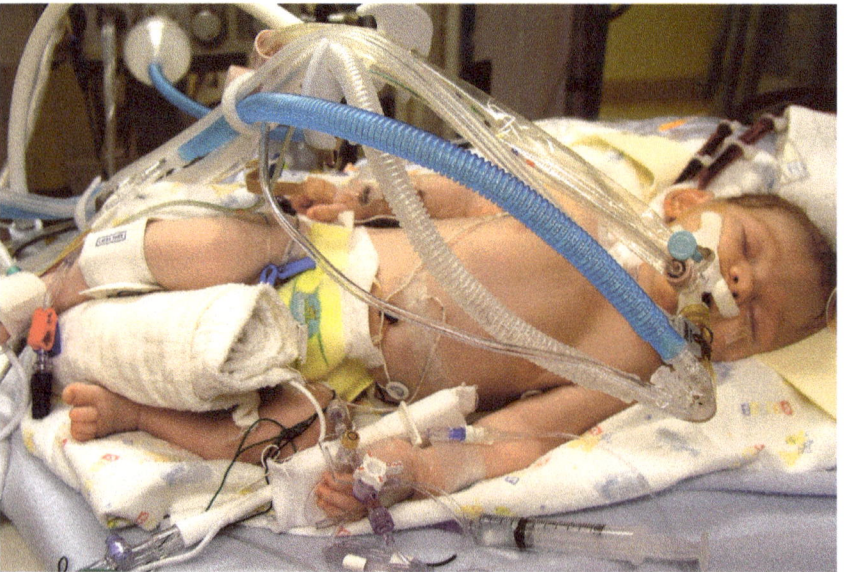

Kieran (we were still calling him Pike at this point) is one day old. He is surrounded by all the equipment needed to keep him alive (top) and a close-up view (bottom).

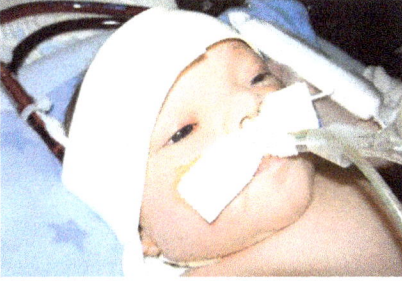

At three days old Kieran would open his eyes for the first time briefly. His night nurses had temporarily weaned him off some of his paralytic medication and took this photo. We cherished this picture as we would not see his eyes open in person for several more days.

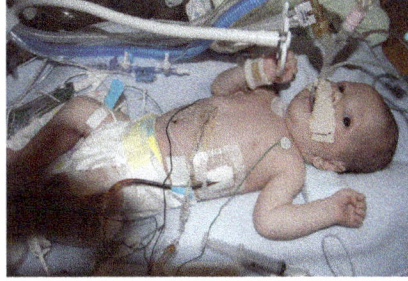

Here he is twelve days old just after his first diaphragm repair but still on ECMO.

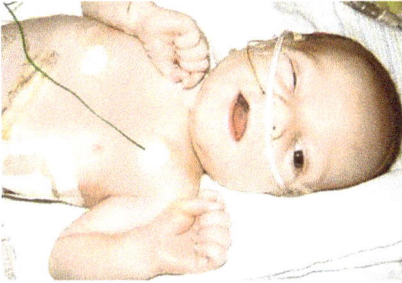

Kieran is just over three weeks. He had just been taken off ECMO and the ventilator and now using just a nasal cannula to help him breathe. We joked that it looks like he's winking at the nurses.

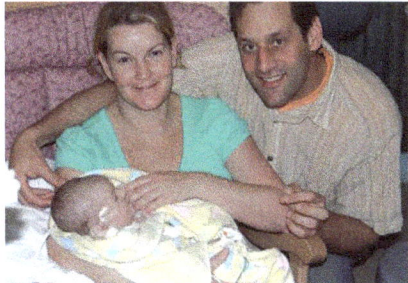

We could finally hold Kieran for the first time. Though he was still attached to many tubes and beeping machines, we couldn't have been happier to hold him in our arms.

July 3, the day Kieran came home. He was nine weeks old and seemed thrilled to be outside in the world. You can see his feeding tube hanging down from the tree. We are celebrating with a bottle of champagne and our dog Chase.

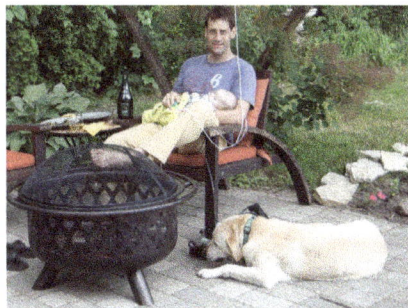

PART TWO
Surviving to Thriving

Our personal life collides with our work. Would we be up to the challenge? We share key principles from our work as human potential coaches, what we learned about each, and how they impacted our journey.

In our work, we've seen these same principles applied to support families, teams and organizations of various kinds. We also share some of those stories.

3

Expand Your Comfort Zone

Rosalind "Roz" Savage, the British ocean rower, holds several Guinness World Records including being the first woman to row solo across three oceans. In her book, *Stop Drifting, Start Rowing*, she talks about her success, she says:

> *Stepping outside your comfort zone is supposed to feel uncomfortable because we're in new and unfamiliar territory. Being uncomfortable is a sign of success, not of failure! So, if we are uncomfortably outside our comfort zones, then that means we are growing. And that is cause for celebration!*[2]

Kieran coming home certainly put us into a place of discomfort.

One of the difficult obstacles for us was how our life rushed back to meet us. When Kieran was at the hospital it felt as though the rest of our life was separate from his fight for survival. Our challenge to manage our own lives and integrate back into the world brought us way outside our comfort zone.

In the past we both equated our comfort zone mostly with our willingness to push physical boundaries where fear was based on the

---

[2] Roz Savage. *Stop Drifting, Start Rowing*. (New York, NY: Hay House, 2013).

consequences of physical injury. Now, the fear was not of a physical risk, but an emotional-social one. Were we going to be able to able to show up as competent parents for Kieran? Would we find a way to fully support our now-expanded family? We were scared.

The amount of learning we each had to step into was overwhelming. It also became apparent that in order to fully support Kieran in the way we wanted, we would have to change significantly from the people we were before. The quote by French literary critic Charles Du Bos kept sticking with us: "The important thing is this, to be willing at any moment to give up who you are for what you could become."

Not knowing how to manage and take care of a sick child would bring up fears we didn't know we had. We didn't know how to do this. We would need to be willing to learn and to learn fast.

Moira: Out In The World

It's easy to focus on Kieran's time in the hospital as the big story. Just getting to survival was huge, and naturally all our focus and energy was on that first critical piece.

What we didn't realize was that the real challenges and learning would start once Kieran came home. We went from having two full-time nurses and an entire care team at the hospital who did everything for him, to suddenly, everything was in our hands. We had spent the last few months giving up control and focusing on just being there. Overnight we had to shift and engage in a whole new way.

I imagine it's a common experience for any first-time parent to feel unprepared and maybe somewhat anxious when they first bring a child home. We had a few additional challenges.

When Kieran came home, he was addicted to morphine and other narcotics that we would have to slowly wean him off, he needed a continuous high flow of oxygen and a full-time feeding tube to keep him alive, and he had an intense personality that was exacerbated by his early experiences.

After the initial excitement and joy that Kieran had survived, and we realized he would actually be coming home, my thoughts were something like "Oh no! How are we supposed to do this? How can the clinical team think we can handle this? After everything he's been through and all it's taken to get him to this point, what if I give him the wrong medication or not enough oxygen or don't get the right amount of food in his feeding tube?"

The fears were many.

One of those fears I didn't realize I had revealed itself as soon as I took Kieran out of the house.

It was clear from the start that Kieran loved to be out in the world. When we went on walks, he would look around, eyes wide as can be, taking everything in with a huge smile on his face. If we didn't get out of the house by 8:00 a.m., he would start acting up, clearly letting me know he wanted to be out and engaging in life.

Going out wasn't easy though. We had to gather Kieran's feeding tube that would beep constantly and had stinky formula that often spilled out. His oxygen requirements meant lugging a large oxygen tank around that was twice the size of Kieran and that is typically used by someone more elderly.

Like many babies, Kieran's mood would shift rapidly. In Kieran's case, the typical baby stuff was exacerbated by symptoms of narcotics withdrawal and the extreme reflux and other physical issues he dealt with constantly. He would go from smiling and interacting happily with everyone to screaming intensely and puking up green bile in a matter of seconds. And this kid could scream. His screams were intense and sounded like something from a horror film. His smiles and laughter were intense too, though, and people couldn't help but get drawn in. I could never predict when or how the screaming and puking would happen, only that it would.

Erik and I were both intentional about not wanting Kieran's condition to define his experience in the world. We thought that meant that we should integrate him into our world. We tried to act as though he was like any other healthy child. So I brought him with me to coffee shop meetings with students and colleagues.

The first time we went to a coffee shop, I gathered all his gear—the feeding tube, the oxygen tank, the medications—and off we went. We did well at first. He smiled his huge smile at everyone and watched everything intently with his big dark eyes. People relaxed despite all the medical equipment and smiled back. After a short time though, he started his intense screaming and bile puking routine. Even polite Minnesotans couldn't help but stare. As a polite Scottish-Minnesotan myself, this was my worst nightmare, causing all that attention and (what I perceived to be) extreme judgment of me as a parent.

My first instinct was to pick the kid up, get out of there as fast as I could, and stay home for the next several years until Kieran (hopefully) got stronger and healthier. That would have been the easy and comfortable choice. Maybe even the polite and respectful choice for the coffee shop patrons.

I eventually realized though, that my intense desire to run was about my fear of being judged as a parent and my desire to keep myself and the other adults in the room comfortable. It certainly was not what was best for Kieran. It wouldn't do anything to help him get from surviving to thriving. More likely, it would prevent that from happening.

I would have to learn that instead of bringing Kieran into our world, I needed to be willing to enter his. To let him dictate what he was ready for and when, and to be willing at any moment to shift course. It was uncomfortable. As parents, we thought we should have the answers and know what was best for our child. Instead, I would have to let go of the desire to control even the smallest tasks and be willing to learn from our newborn if we were going to help him survive and thrive.

The practice of letting go during my pregnancy would serve me well again now that Kieran had come home. I needed to find a way to acknowledge, and then let go of, the very real and many fears. I realized that if I held on to them, it wouldn't serve any of us. If I let those fears drive my behavior and my interactions with Kieran, he certainly wouldn't feel safe and loved. He would more likely take on my fears. Given what he'd already been through, that was the last thing I wanted to put on him.

Parenting Kieran would constantly force me to choose between staying comfortable and being willing to step into the discomfort to learn and grow. Up to this point, I thought of learning as primarily an intellectual activity. Kieran would force me to realize that real learning, the kind that would allow me to show up differently in the world, required so much more.

Outside the Comfort Zone

Kieran's diagnosis pushed us out of our comfort zone in a very different way than we had experienced in the past. This was more than a physical or intellectual discomfort. Kieran's diagnosis forced us to a new place emotionally than either of us had been before, to a new kind of discomfort and fear.

What is the comfort zone really? And why is it so hard to be outside it, either by choice or circumstance?

The comfort zone is a concept of a psychological space (or mindset) that looks different for everyone. The Merriam-Webster dictionary definition of comfort zone is "the level at which one functions with ease and familiarity." It provides a state of mental security and low anxiety.

There's certainly nothing wrong with that. Humans naturally gravitate to the comfort zone. It's safe there, there's no nervousness, and confidence resides there. The comfort zone is useful. It's efficient and doesn't require much emotional or intellectual energy. The outcome is usually already known with little chance of failure.

When we ask people what it feels like inside their comfort zone, they say things like "predictable, known outcome, safe, repetitive." Certainly, none of those things were true for us after Kieran's diagnosis. The patterns that worked yesterday were not going to work going forward.

The Learning Zone

How much learning happens inside the comfort zone? Typically, not much. Little tweaks here and there show up in the comfort zone, but usually no new ideas or information. That wouldn't work for us with Kieran and it likely won't work well with the pace of change in the world today.

In our work, we see that when people are willing to go through the discomfort required to take action within fear, they experience exhilaration and joy on the other side. This same cycle became a rhythm for us in our journey with Kieran. Experience fear and maybe dread, find a way to act anyhow, and many times feel relief or exhilaration on the other side.

We found it critical to be willing to get outside the comfort zone, not just physically and intellectually, but emotionally as well in order to learn with—and from—Kieran. Research confirms that it's when uncertainty or discomfort exists that people are primed for learning.[3]

We call that space outside the comfort zone "the learning zone." Getting to the learning zone requires moving outside the comfort zone in all the domains of human experience—intellect, body and emotion.

The challenge, of course, is that it doesn't feel good to be in the learning zone, especially as adults. Adults typically don't like to fail. In this culture there are strong stories about how failing is bad or weak, when in actuality it is a key component to learning.

In our work as human potential coaches and facilitators, we experience that people are not necessarily afraid of change; rather, they are scared of being incompetent on the other side of change. As a result, they push back on the change or the issue, rather than explore their fear. Measurements of success and reward are often based on competence. People get paid to be competent. This makes it more difficult to say, "I don't know."

Choosing to be out of the comfort zone, or being forced out, is hard work. Humans are hardwired to stay there and to stay safe. The learning zone is where fears are exposed. It is scary, unknown and unpredictable. Strange things start to happen. The heart beats faster, palms can get sweaty, human biology takes over. The body screams at you to get back into the comfort zone.

Enter the amygdala, the region of the brain that allows us to feel fear and trigger a rapid response. In the 1930s, two famous neuroscientists, Heinrich Klüver and Paul Bucy, surgically removed the amygdala (and temporal lobes) from monkeys and discovered that they exhibited behavior that implied they had no fear and were indifferent toward

---

[3] Robert A. Burton. *On Being Certain: Believing You Are Right Even When You're Not.* (New York, NY: St. Martin's Press, 2008).

humans. This could be helpful in some cases, but dangerous for survival in others.

Stepping outside the comfort zone causes the amygdala to fire and scream, "Get back in there—it's not safe out here. *You might die!*" That region of the brain is designed to keep us safe.[4] It served humans well when fighting other Neanderthals and wild animals. It's designed to continually be on high alert and detect threats in order to survive. We affectionately refer to the amygdala and associated regions of the brain as our *lizard brain* because of its important role in our early evolution.

The lizard brain is on high alert all the time and it doesn't distinguish between a physical and an emotional threat. Getting in a conflict with someone fires the same biological reaction that would occur if there was a saber tooth tiger about to attack, or when we are in physical danger. In today's world, humans are constantly fighting our biology. With increased awareness, the lizard brain can be managed and tapped into, rather than letting it drive undesired behaviors.

Although popular concepts, the reality of fearless living and being without fear may not be appropriate for everyone. Without the emotion of fear and the ability to react quickly to threat stimuli, we wouldn't be alive. Our colleague, Larry Burback, likes to say: "If you don't feel fear, you are dangerous to yourself and the people around you."

The question is not are you afraid or uncomfortable. The question is are you going to let that fear get in the way? Or, are you going to acknowledge it and move through it? The challenge is whether you can take an action while feeling that fear. As author and researcher Brené Brown says: "One of the worst things we can do is pretend fear and uncertainty don't exist."[5]

---

[4] Ralph Adolphs. "The Biology of Fear." *Current Biology*. 23(2) (2013): R79–R93. Cell Press.

[5] Brené Brown. *Rising Strong: The Reckoning. The Rumble. The Revolution.* (New York, NY: Simon Walker, 2015).

Sometimes the fear is appropriate, and the response should be to listen to it and respond because of it. In fact, the next step beyond the learning zone is the terror zone—a place where the fear is so great and stress so high that no learning will happen and irreparable (physical or emotional) damage could occur.

More often though, fears can get in the way of the things you care most about. They cause you to miss out on the joy and exhilaration on the other side of fear. They certainly would get in the way for us on our journey with Kieran.

The challenge is to let go of the desire to be right or to not fail when attempting something new. The opportunity is to go into each new experience from a place of wonderment and curiosity. Even the most challenging experiences can be entered in from that place. It's not easy, but it is possible.

Moving from the comfort zone to the learning zone requires a mental shift. Acknowledging that you are a beginner creates an opportunity to learn. Resisting the urge to show up as if you were already competent, makes it easier to navigate the challenges. The more you have experiences outside your comfort zone, the more your comfort zone expands. What once was not comfortable now is.

On the other hand, the opposite is also true. If you do not have new experiences outside the comfort zone, it shrinks. What once was comfortable no longer is. The comfort zone decreases along with new possibilities.

If learning is something you seek out, something you value as an important life experience, then seeking discomfort is critical to success.

For us, viewing our journey with Kieran through the filter of learning allowed us to relax more in each moment and view the messiness as opportunities to learn. We messed up often with each other and with Kieran. There were many tense moments and heated arguments where we let our exhaustion and fear take over. We had to work at reminding ourselves we were beginners and messing up was part of the journey, a way to learn.

We had to constantly pay attention when we wanted to retreat or control—was it our lizard brain? Was it a useful fear or our biology getting in the way of what might be possible? We had to continually ask ourselves, is this decision taking care of our fear or letting Kieran (and us) play on the edges to learn? We would have to mess up over and over to find where those edges were.

Stepping into the Learning Zone

Lynn was a highly successful executive in investment banking. Her colleagues praised Lynn's work ethic, drive and integrity. Through that hard work and commitment to her team she continued to rise through the organization, eventually to the Chief Financial Officer (CFO) role.

We met Lynn in the midst of the financial crisis in 2008. She was the lone female member of her company's leadership team. Like many firms at the time, her organization felt like they were in a defensive position and were "back on their heels, simply reacting to the crisis." Their desire was to find a way to get out in front and be more proactive about their fate within all the uncertainty.

Lynn had a critical role in that journey and recognized that what she had been doing up to this point, the behaviors that had served her well and gotten her to where she was, weren't going to work for her in this new chaotic environment.

Lynn and her team went through an awareness process where we created an "outside the comfort zone" experience designed to expose what was showing up on their team at work. Lynn talks about one of the significant learnings for her from this experience:

> *The concept of comfort zone and learning zone helped me to distinguish what I was scared of, versus what I didn't want to do. Before experiencing this concept, I lumped fear in with not wanting to do something. This limited the opportunities in front of me as a person and as a leader. Once I was able to recognize*

fear for what it was, an opportunity to learn, a new world of possibility opened up.

I was now able to choose courage more often, step into discomfort and feel the exhilaration of accomplishment on the other side. It allowed me to move from a transactional CFO to a more strategic CFO. It shifted how my team responded—we could all be more proactive rather than reactive.

As a result, I was able to bring more value to the organization as a whole, and enjoy the journey more. Shifting my focus to expanding my comfort zone by being willing to step into the learning zone, helped me to be more vulnerable and authentic in my relationships, both at work and home.

In one of the leadership team meetings Lynn stepped way outside her comfort zone and shared her vulnerability. During a highly emotional dialogue around the work they were doing as a team, despite coaching from others not to do so, she let herself express her emotions and she started to cry.

To this day I am not exactly sure why I started to cry other than the lack of integrity I was having between who I was and what I was trying to be (a tough, uber-confident CFO of a financial services firm) and a significant lack of confidence in myself. Did the stress of the financial crisis play its part in all of this? I am sure it did.

At first, she felt embarrassed, which made her cry more. Then she took a breath and expressed her thoughts and concerns about how she was struggling with feeling like she had an equal place and role on the leadership team given what she perceived as a lack of certain key experiences. To her surprise, the rest of the team, all men, supported her. Instead of mocking or avoiding her feelings they acknowledged the gift that she just gave the team. The reality was, they were all scared, navigating their own concerns and fears. Lynn had simply voiced how she had been feeling for months but felt unable to express.

In her willingness to be uncomfortable and vulnerable, Lynn opened up the space for her team to have the hard conversations they had been avoiding for months. With that one gesture, she created a deep connection with the team, allowing them to support each other and move toward shared commitments that they were previously unable to accomplish. Stepping into the learning zone revealed her courage and inspired the rest of the team to open up, acknowledge their own fears, and take actions that were not available to them before now.

Consider This

Where are you allowing fear to get in the way of what is possible? What are the consequences for not taking action?

Fig 3. *Our Lizard (brain) explains the reasons not to venture outside the fence.*

4

The Power Of Choice

From 1942 to 1945 psychiatrist Viktor Frankl worked in four different Nazi concentration camps, including Auschwitz, while his parents, brother and pregnant wife perished. Frankl had an opportunity to leave Austria just before the Hitler occupation. He instead chose to stay and be with his elderly parents, knowing their probable fate and his.

In his 1946 book *Man's Search for Meaning*,[6] Frankl describes his experiences in the concentration camp and his approach to psychotherapy. Frankl argues (from his own experiences and those of his patients) that "we cannot avoid suffering, but we can choose how we cope with it. We can find meaning in it and move forward with renewed purpose."

Our son's diagnosis challenged us to look for the choice and not fall into blame and resentment. The concept of choice often challenged us to look inside ourselves and sometimes we didn't like what we found. We recognize we're not responsible for everything that happens in our lives, but as Frankl's experience so clearly illustrates, we do have a choice in how we respond to even the most dire of circumstances.

---

[6] Victor E. Frankl. *Man's Search for Meaning: An Introduction to Logotherapy*. (New York, NY: Simon & Schuster, 1946).

Erik: On Choice

Before Kieran's diagnosis my life had not been impacted much by Moira's pregnancy. I was detached and not yet connected to the child growing inside of Moira. I did not fully appreciate the impact it had on her and the experience she was having.

The doctor telling us that our baby had a severe case of CDH created a new level of awareness around what mattered to me. Up until that point, I was taking the pregnancy and the approaching birth for granted. It was going to happen. I felt disconnected and mainly continued to focus on myself. While I recognized I actively participated in making the pregnancy happen, I felt like I didn't have any choice or role in the pregnancy itself. The diagnosis changed my view on that.

The diagnosis presented a choice that Moira and I needed to make that I could never have imagined having to make as a parent. The doctor's perspective was that the impact of the diagnosis would be so negative to our family's quality of life that it wasn't worth continuing the pregnancy.

Although the doctor's perspective was well grounded and supported by the existing data, the choice was still ours to make. How do you make that choice? The choice to continue or end a life for someone who can't make that choice for himself—for someone whose life might be unimaginably challenging?

It may be a really obvious choice for some people. Some might even believe they already know what choice they would make, even if they've never been in that situation. That wasn't true for us. Even if we did think we knew ahead of time, everything was different when we were in the actual experience.

I couldn't imagine anyone making that choice for us. Nor would I presume to know what is best for any other parent in that situation, or in any other for that matter.

How would I feel if we decided to terminate the pregnancy based solely on our doctor's initial recommendation? What level of commitment would show up in me if I did not feel it was my choice to make? Who is responsible for deciding the risk level that is acceptable for another human? What if our baby's quality of life turned out to be as low as they told us it could be?

These questions were not easy to grapple with. If we delayed the decision or focused on whether it was the "right" one, it created hesitation, doubt, and eventually someone else or the circumstance would have decided for us.

They were our decisions to make, and if they came from someone else the risk of anger and resentment would be too high a consequence that I would have to live with, whichever side of the decision we landed.

Owning our choice changed my view on all things moving forward. Owning that choice allowed me to be open to the learning that would show up when things became challenging. I had no one else to blame or resent for where we were. I had fully chosen in, and all I could do now was be in it and look for the learning regardless of what showed up along the way.

My relationship with the pregnancy changed from "that thing growing inside Moira's stomach," to "I want to be in a relationship with that child right now." I became fully invested in the journey. I was now aware that the only relationship I may have with our child was between then and his birth. There was no guarantee of anything beyond that. I was going to do whatever it took to take advantage of the time I did have with our soon-to-be-born child.

I experienced the impact of choosing in. Life happens. Circumstances happen, and the power resides in how I choose to respond.

Living In Choice

Many people go through life believing that, for the most part, they have choices. Yet in many circumstances they use the language of "I have to." I have to go to work, I have to bring my kids to their event, I have to get that project done. I have to pay taxes. There is usually not even an awareness of what language they're using. "I have to" is just the default.

To illustrate, try this short experience:

First, think of all the things you do in your life that you feel you have to do. That is the language you use. I have to go to work, I have to pick up my kids, I have to go to the family event, I have to pay my taxes.

Keep thinking and make a list in your head. Take a minute and keep the list going. If it's a short list, repeat it over again.

Now identify the emotions that you are feeling right now. What are they?

Most people will identify words such as: stressful, anxious, loss of control, anger, frustration, apathy, fatigue, resentment, and so on.

Now, erase that list in your head and make a new one. Think of all the things that you choose to do. Again, that is the language you use. It might be some of the same things as in your "have to" list. I choose to hang with my friends. I choose to play golf. I choose to go on a vacation.

Take another minute to keep that list going. If it's a short list, repeat it over again.

What are the emotions you are feeling now?

For most people, this list will be more along the lines of feelings such as: freedom, energetic, happy, empowered, excited, energized, etc.

Common feelings / emotions generated from "Have To" and "Choose To"	
I Have To...	**I Choose To...**
Stress	Freedom
Overwhelm	Joy
Lack of control	Empowered
Anger	Energized
Resentment	Motivated

Now, look at the two columns. Which column is a place that you'd rather spend most of your time? Silly question, right? Yet many times, you may not even notice the internal conversation that you're having. It just runs on autopilot.

If you are spending most of your time in a "have to" conversation, it's very likely that the emotions in the left column are what's showing up in your life. If you're in a "choose to" conversation more often, then it is likely that the emotions in the right column are the ones that show up more consistently in your life.

For many, the "have to" conversation happens more often than a "choose to" conversation without having awareness of it. Making the switch is empowering.

Using "have to" language does serve a purpose. It can be used as an excuse so that when the outcome is not what is desired, then it can be used to shift responsibility to someone else because "I had to do it."

Making a choice creates ownership of the outcome, creating empowerment for the person making the choice. Owning the outcome can take you outside the comfort zone because it can make you feel exposed and unsafe.

Choices communicate what a person cares about. Revealing who you are can cause you to feel vulnerable. Using "have to" can help create a false armor, making you feel safe and protecting you from having to answer why you made that choice.

It is not written on a cave wall somewhere that you always have a choice. It is a point of view, a place to be aware of where the pattern is for you. The question is where do you spend most of your time? Where is the pattern in your life?

Moira: Challenging Choices

There were many times after Kieran came home where all of the "have to" emotions would show up for me. Erik was often traveling for work and getting his business off the ground. It seemed every time he left town we would end up in the hospital for something—Kieran's feeding tube coming out or another surgery. My internal dialogue often went something like "why does Erik get to continue his life, and mine is so dramatically interrupted?" Overwhelm and resentment would creep in more often than I care to admit.

I didn't always handle it well and would often blame Erik. It certainly wasn't Erik's fault. He was doing all he could to make the business work for our family and was in a place of overwhelm himself. He would quickly offer to switch places with me and I know it broke his heart every time he left or couldn't be there in the hospital with us. Once, Erik was working with a leadership team in France and Kieran ended up in the hospital. Erik recalls, "I couldn't focus on the work. All I could think about was my family and that I desperately wanted to be there with you and Kieran. I would have changed spots with you in a second."

In reality, there was no way I was not going to be with my child in the hospital. Kieran needed me and I wanted to be there with him. I *chose* to be there. I slowly learned to pay attention when resentment and overwhelm would show up and look for where the choice was. It didn't make the hard choices any easier or make the emotions disappear; but it was a tool that helped me to check in, get clear about the choices I was making, and take ownership over them, rather than go to blame and resentment.

Good and Bad Choices

People often talk about choices as being "good" or "bad" and get into an internal dialogue of "right" and "wrong." Really, though, you don't determine a choice was good or bad until after the outcome of that choice. It is a look back on what transpired. Most people don't wake up saying "I'm going to make more bad choices today." Most make choices based on the best interpretation of the information (intellectual and emotional) they have at the time.

When we were making the choice to continue the pregnancy, we had no idea at the time if it was a good choice or bad choice. It was the best choice we could make for us with the information we had at the time. The clinical and emotional data. For someone else, the same information could have easily led to a different, appropriate for them, choice. Labeling a choice as "good" or "bad" at the time we make it is driven by our fear of the future outcome that we can't yet determine.

The language of "good and bad" or "right and wrong" can be debilitating and can stop you from making an active choice. Sometimes there are multiple choices and none of them are desirable. Life happens. By not making a choice, someone or something else will make it for you. Life doesn't stop as a result of being scared of making a decision.

Taking good or bad out of the conversation makes it easier to see that it's just a choice with an opportunity to learn from it once a result is achieved. Make a choice, get a result, receive new information and make another choice.

In our journey with our son, the concept around choice allowed us to make one choice at a time—to look for what is the next choice we can make, rather than focusing on the entire journey and feeling overwhelmed by it.

It can be easy to use "have to" as an excuse. It's a way to not take ownership of the results. If the result is not the one you want, you can say, "I had to do it, it wasn't my choice. It's not the decision I would have made." It makes it easier to not be invested in the outcome. "Don't look at me, I had to do it."

It's easy to fall into using language like "I can't" instead of "I won't." Using "I can't" puts it out of your hands. It is disempowering, it's not a choice. Fear of being vulnerable often drives the use of "I can't."

"I won't" is a choice that reflects what a person cares about and lives within them. It can be an engine to empower your life.

For us, this story is not about the choice of whether to have Kieran or not. The story is about our next choice. Once we committed to staying in the journey with Kieran, we had to decide, "How we were going to show up for him and are we willing to learn?"

Consider This

Pay attention to the language you use in your life. Are there places where you believe you have no choice and use the language "I have to"? What might be different if you came from the perspective of "I choose to"?

Fig 4. Horse looks for where the choice is.

5

Adjust Your Filter

On May 6, 1954, Roger Bannister ran one mile in three minutes, fifty-nine and four-tenths of a second, becoming the first person to run the mile under four minutes. Before Bannister's record-breaking run, many in the public and scientific community believed it was *physiologically impossible* for a human to run that fast.

When Bannister finished the race he said, "Doctors and scientists said that breaking the four-minute mile was impossible, that one would die in the attempt. Thus, when I got up from the track after collapsing at the finish line, I figured I was dead."

In John Bryant's book *3:59.4: The Quest to Break the Four-Minute Mile*, he recalls that despite scientific beliefs, runners had been chasing the elusive four-minute mile since at least 1886. He notes: "It had become as much a psychological barrier as a physical one. And like an unconquerable mountain the closer it was approached, the more daunting it seemed."[7]

---

[7] John Bryant. *3:59.4. The Quest to Break the 4-minute Mile*. (New York, NY: Penguin Random House, 2005).

The four-minute barrier stood for decades despite numerous talented athletes training relentlessly. Then, just forty-six days after Bannister's performance, both Bannister and John Landy broke the barrier again and ran even faster. Just over a year later three runners broke the barrier in the same race. Over 1,400 runners have since broken that once "scientifically impossible" barrier and the current world record is well under four minutes at 3:43.13.

In their book *The Power of Impossible Thinking*, Yoram Wind and Colin Crook analyzed possible contributions to Bannister's performance as they wondered what was behind it:

> *Was there a sudden growth spurt in human evolution? Was there a genetic engineering experiment that created a new race of super runners? No. What changed was the mental model. The runners of the past had been held back by a mindset that said they could not surpass the four-minute mile. When that limit was broken, the others saw that they could do something they had previously thought impossible.[8]*

Humans all have their own belief systems and filters through which they see the world that influence what's possible in their lives. Margaret Wheatley, esteemed author and organizational consultant, explained the impact of belief systems in a 2001 article.

> *Many years ago, Joel Barker popularized the notion of paradigms or worldviews, those beliefs and assumptions through which we see the world and explain its processes. He stated that when something is impossible to achieve with one view of the world, it can be surprisingly easy to accomplish with a new one. I have found this to be*

---

[8] Yoram (Jerry) Wind and Colin Crook. *The Power of Impossible Thinking: Transform the Business of Your Life and the Life of Your Business* (Upper Saddle River, New Jersey: Prentice Hall, 2006).

delightfully true. Now that I understand people and organizations as living systems, filled with the innovative dynamics characteristic of all life, many intractable problems have become solvable.[9]

For us, Kieran would provide a mirror to expose our own filters and challenge our beliefs on a daily basis.

Moira: My Shifting Filter

I'm sitting in a faculty meeting observing a heated discussion about resources and the direction of our department in the next year. Typically, I would have jumped in with my opinion and fought for a fair share of resources for my students and our lab.

Today though, I just couldn't engage. I had just left Kieran with my mother that morning to come in just for this meeting, which I felt was critically important.

Kieran was having a particularly challenging morning. He had been throwing up green bile more than usual and his feeding tube was acting up and beeping nonstop. Even on the best days, my mom disliked dealing with his "bloody feeding tube" as she called it with her heavy Scottish accent. She was a saint for caring for him, anyhow. When I left Kieran, he screamed his intense scream that always caused a physical reaction in me making it nearly impossible to leave. The meeting was important, though, so I left.

I'm sitting there watching the heated discussion thinking, "What am I doing here? This is an incredible waste of energy right now. I should be home with Kieran." It was never more clear to me that I needed to change something.

[9] Margaret J. Wheatly. "Innovation Means Relying on Everyone's Creativity: Leader to Leader," Spring 2001. Accessed November 11, 2019 https://www.margaretwheatley.com/articles/innovationmeans.html.

It should have been an easy fix. Just leave. Go home. Be with your child. Of course, it didn't seem that easy to me. I had just gone through the process of receiving a promotion and tenure. After graduate school, post-doctoral fellowships, publications and grants, and various moves, I was now, finally, a tenured associate professor at a University in a city where I wanted to be living. I had a great lab, wonderful students and collaborators, solid funding, and excellent benefits.

And yet, it wasn't working for me right now.

It wasn't just my desire to be home with Kieran. I had gradually started to see that the type of work I really wanted to do was going to be challenging from within the confines of academia. I had a desire to bring what we were learning in our research to the community and support people in a more sustainable way than grant funding alone allowed for.

It was time to make a change. But what?

My filter was informed by the belief that people don't leave tenured positions. I had certainly never heard of it happening. Plus, I had worked so hard and I wanted to do meaningful work. I also had to consider that Erik was an entrepreneur and we had zero financial safety net and no benefits if I left. There was also the challenge of wondering about what kind of work I would do. I'd spent my career in academia with the assumption that was where I would stay. I would have to make it work.

Erik had a different experience and perspective. His filter was informed by his experiences as an entrepreneur. In his mind, I could do whatever work I wanted to. There were endless possibilities. We just had to be willing to do the work and make it happen.

There were many beliefs I had to shift. As an academic my filter was informed by the perception that businesses were focused on financial results and less on doing good in the world. I argued with Erik without really being curious about his perspective. I thought he just didn't get it. I was convinced that there were no other good options for me.

Over time, I started to see that there might be a different path—that what I perceived as freedom in my current career was really boxing me into something that wasn't working for me individually or for our family as a whole. I realized that creating a business could serve as a platform to do meaningful work while also creating the freedom I desired.

It felt like there were so many risks to leaving my current role—risks to any financial security, risks to my identity and potential impact in the world. In the end, none of those compared to my desire to be fully available and present for Kieran. Eventually I would leave my tenured position and forge a different path. It would be one of the most uncomfortable, challenging, and ultimately rewarding decisions of my life. It allowed me the possibility to have the impact I wanted and the freedom to support my family in the way I desired.

Your Filter

Have you ever taken the time to explore what influences how you see the world—your filter? Your filter does a great job of helping you navigate your life. It keeps you safe by filtering out irrelevant information and providing a way to make quick judgements about people and situations. Many people aren't aware of the impact their filter has on their decisions and actions—subconsciously filtering out information quietly behind the scene.

What influences your filter? Largely, it's influenced by your experiences in the world, the culture and generation you grew up in. Filters create coherency and a confirmation of what is real. At the same time, these differing perspectives often create conflict, frustration and division. Each person's filter is different and just as real as the next.

Left unexplored, these differences can get in the way of quality relationships and can prevent honest dialogue, learning, and collaboration. By paying attention to what impacts your filter, stepping back and getting curious about other people (rather than trying to be right), new perspectives can be exposed: learning where intersections are with others, helping to better understand what might be getting in the way of relationships or the ability to collaborate.

We like to say that nobody owns the truth, but everybody owns a piece of it. It's often only when you open up to someone else's perspective that new possibilities reveal themselves.

Your filter has great value in ensuring that you make decisions that line up with what you say is important. It keeps you safe. Your filter supports you in many ways, and if you are not aware of how it functions, it can get in the way of helping you achieve what you want in life. Just as your filter creates your interpretation of reality, it can also confuse you into considering your reality as truth when it is not.

You are constantly bombarded with information, and at the same time you are hard-wired to determine quickly what does not line up or resonate with your current version of reality. As a result, when you are confronted with a different point of view, you can feel threatened and be pushed outside of your comfort zone, firing that darn amygdala again.

Increasing awareness of your filter can feel uncomfortable because it can feel like a threat to who you are and what you care about. Your filter allows you to find your way in the world. It is influenced by both your conscious and unconscious mind.

You are taking in a high influx of data at any given time, yet can only focus on a small amount each moment. Your filter is constantly at work, deciding what is relevant. That prehistoric part of the brain is really good at filtering out any information it thinks is extraneous. You take in roughly 11,000,000 bits of information through your senses every second and only consciously process about fifty bits.[10] The rest is still there, available in the unconscious mind, where it sits ready to influence your behavior unknowingly.

What happens when somebody you've never met walks in the room? Most of the time you will instantly make judgements: "I like her. I don't like him. I trust/don't trust that person." That's your filter acting automatically and often even without your awareness. As a human, you are constantly making judgments unconsciously and automatically through your filter.

The reality of the world you see is not the whole reality; it is only part of it. It is your interpretation of reality, based on how your filter has screened data by looking for those elements that support your existing point of view. This filtering function directly impacts all your decisions and the actions you take.

There are many contributors to determining your filter at any given time. For example:

- Gender
- Race
- Where you were born
- Where you live now
- Historical experiences

---

[10] "New Measure of Human Brain Processing Speed." *MIT Technology Review*. August 25, 2009. Accessed November 11, 2019 https://www.technologyreview.com/s/415041/new-measure-of-human-brain-processing-speed/.

- Current mindset/mood
- People in your sphere of influence
- Your current beliefs

Increasing your awareness and understanding of how each of these impacts how you see the world will open up choices for you to see new possibilities. It can be a tough journey to challenge yourself—to look in the mirror to see what currently exists. What brought you here could be the very thing getting in the way of where you want to go next. Your willingness to explore your filter is crucial to your ability to learn, grow, and cultivate the relationships that are most important to you. It will impact the choices available to you and your life fulfillment. Exploring your filter can be challenging, taking you outside your comfort zone, easily putting you into defense mode, rather than a curious one.

At the heart of understanding your filter is the level of awareness you have of yourself. You can only be aware of what is around you to the extent that you are aware of what is inside you.

Incremental Learning

When you take an action it generates a result. In an effort to take effective action you may do research, analyze, put projections together, and then make a decision. The decision guides the actions that you take, and those actions generate a result.

Sometimes those results are not what you wanted to have happen. To get a different result you may take a different action. That would be an effective way to adjust and learn and strive for success. There are many processes for this type of learning and adjustment. We call this "incremental learning."

```
┌──────────┐      ┌──────────┐      ┌──────────┐
│ beliefs  │ ⇒   │  action  │ ⇒   │  result  │
└──────────┘      └──────────┘      └──────────┘
        │                                │
        └──── Incremental Learning ──────┘
```

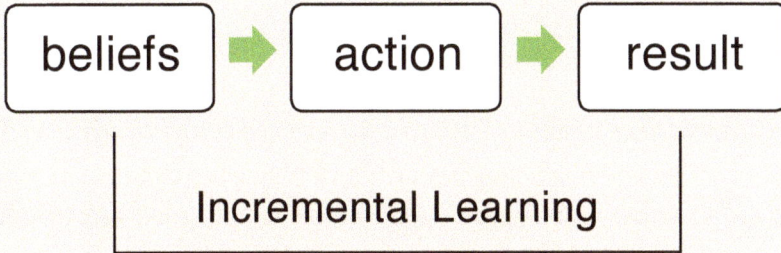

In incremental learning, your current beliefs inform the actions available to you.

Breakthrough Learning

What determines what actions you have available? Does one person have different actions available than another person?

The actions available to you are largely determined by your existing belief systems which influence your filter.

What if you were able to take a step back and observe those beliefs, challenge them and explore them? What if you were open to another person's beliefs, or a different industry's perspective? This could open up a set of actions available to you that you may not have seen before.

The challenge with looking at your own beliefs is that your biology takes over and wants to keep you safe. Challenging your belief system does not feel safe. Your filter helps you navigate the world. Your filter helps you feel comfortable with who you are. When your beliefs are challenged, it's easy to go into defense mode and retreat into your comfort zone.

The opportunity is to explore your current belief system to see what may be getting in the way or supporting what you say you care about.

If you're willing to step into the discomfort this requires, new actions can emerge that you didn't see before. Outcomes that you didn't know existed or saw as impossible often become possible.

Stepping out of existing belief systems is a way to quickly and consistently discover new opportunities and adapt to changing circumstances. It first requires that you can see them—that you become aware of what you believe is possible or not—and perceive the ways those beliefs shape your actions. We call this "breakthrough learning." The key is to be curious enough to explore your current belief systems to be able to see new ones.

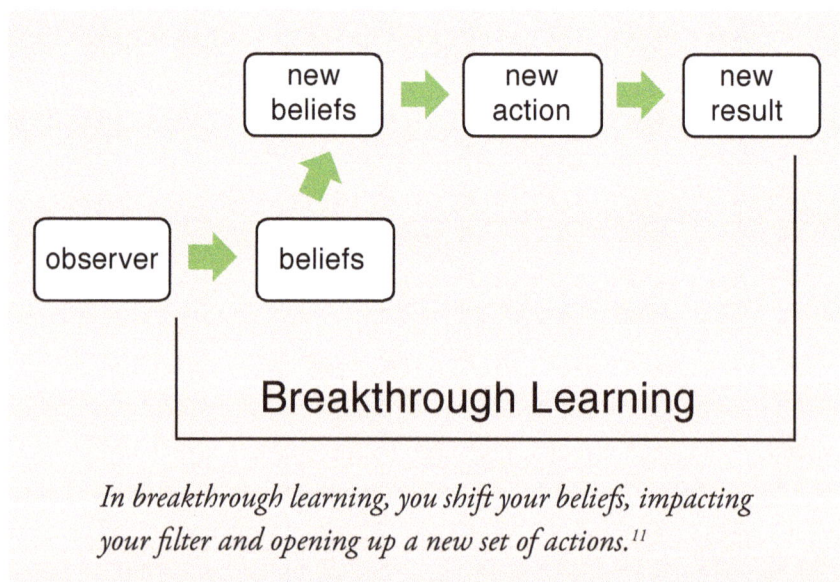

In breakthrough learning, you shift your beliefs, impacting your filter and opening up a new set of actions.[11]

Incremental learning builds from what has worked in the past. It can be useful when you are trying to improve a process or make gains that involve low risk and a higher degree of certainty.

On the other hand, breakthrough learning demands that you open up and step outside your comfort zone and be willing to "not know." It

[11] Gregory Bateson. "The Logical Categories of Learning and Communication." *Steps to an Ecology of Mind* (University of Chicago Press, 1972, 2000).

requires a shift in how you show up from a need to be competent, to being willing to be a beginner. It often requires a willingness to unlearn what you thought you knew and approach life from a place of curiosity. When you practice showing up in a way that facilitates breakthrough learning, it creates new possibilities you did not see before and opens up a set of actions that were previously not available to you.

Success does not usually happen when first taking new actions. That failure becomes an opportunity to learn. You now have new information that did not exist before. This type of learning allows you to break patterns and address the quick pace of change and uncertainty in the world. It is a muscle you can build and repeat where you see the value.

Shifting Belief Systems In Pediatric Pain Management

As Doctor Stefan Friedrichsdorf enters the room, you can sense his passion and energy. He is fully present and focused on the people he's talking to. He has an infectious smile and likes to say "groovy."

When Friedrichsdorf was in medical school, he observed that pediatric patients were often in what he felt was unnecessary pain. In an interview,[12] he notes one particularly revealing experience as a medical resident:

> In Germany, there were no phlebotomists at the time.
> As a young doctor, you had to practice on tiny babies
> to draw their blood every morning and they were
> of course screaming bloody murder. Very quickly, I

---

[12] Lauren Heathcote. "On a Mission to Eradicate Pain and Suffering: A Promise for Better Pediatric Pain Care—A Conversation with Stefan Friedrichsdorf." International Association for the Study of Pain (IASP), Pain Research Forum (August 27, 2018).

realized that I wanted to help make this go away. I noticed I was the one causing the most pain. Most of the time a child's pain is not caused by their disease, but rather by the intervention and their treatment. I thought "This stinks. We can do better."

The prevailing belief at the time was that pediatric patients have under-developed nervous systems and don't actually feel pain, so there's no need to treat it. Even if they do feel pain, it was believed they would never remember those early experiences. Furthermore, there was resistance to providing pain management to children because of a concern that they might become addicted to narcotics, despite a lack of supporting evidence.

Any parent who has taken their baby for a flu shot or first set of immunizations knows that babies feel pain. The prevailing beliefs were so embedded in the clinical world that as recent as the 1980s children still underwent surgery, including open heart surgery, without anesthesia or other pain medications.

After medical school, Dr. Friedrichsdorf had the opportunity to go to Australia for a fellowship with one of the few clinics in the world at the time doing work with pediatric pain medicine and palliative care. "It was so cool," he said. "Here I was taking pain away, rather than inducing it." He was hooked.

Medical practice at the time was fairly siloed. There was so much to know that clinicians were understandably fully consumed just keeping up with the literature in their specialty area. The benefit was that their knowledge ran deep which was critical for successful specialty surgeries and care of complex conditions (like Kieran's). Their knowledge was hard earned and the work they did was critical. Lives were literally at stake with every move. So understandably (and even critically), their beliefs were tightly held and their filters were narrow.

In Australia, they took a more holistic approach to pediatric pain management. From his diverse training, Friedrichsdorf realized that pediatric pain was complex, and he would need to constantly strive to understand a variety of perspectives from fields outside his own expertise. All pediatric clinicians know that babies are not just small adults, so he couldn't just draw from practices in adult pain management.

As he explored the literature in other areas, it turned out that contrary to the current thinking of many, there is actually an *increased* rate of death and more complications in children in the NICU if pain isn't managed. If used correctly, the powerful drugs that many were scared to use in pediatric patients (such as fentanyl which is similar to morphine) are safe even in large doses for children and babies.

Even with substantial quality research and clinical evidence, "existing beliefs are still the biggest barrier," Friedrichsdorf notes; so much so that he spent time learning how to teach adult learners. He now often spends a significant part of his lectures on pediatric pain management on this very topic knowing that even the medical literature won't be enough to get clinicians to make a shift in their practice.

Doctors' belief systems weren't the only challenge. Parents' belief systems impact their children's outcomes too. "In the case of chronic pain and children with primary pain disorders, emerging data seem to support the notion that it becomes a self-fulfilling prophecy whether or not a child becomes pain free," notes Dr. Friedrichsdorf. Research studies[13] now show that parental catastrophic thinking about their child's pain prior to surgery was linked to distressing pain memories for the child months later.

Dr. Friedrichsdorf realized it would require a multi-disciplinary team to truly support not just the children, but also their families. His team now includes physicians, fellows, nurses, practitioners, psychologists, physical therapists, a research and quality improvement team, palliative nurses, social work chaplains, child life specialists, music therapists, clinical nurses, massage therapists, administrative assistants, clinic staff and managers.

Fortunately for us, just a few years before Kieran was born, Friedrichsdorf landed in Minnesota. The leadership team at Children's Minnesota understood they needed to do something different to fully care for their pediatric patients and brought him in to start the first of its kind (in the United States) pediatric pain management and palliative care unit. It took some time to get the clinicians on board, and even years later there is constant (re)educating to do for clinicians and families.

At first, Moira was skeptical of Dr. Friedrichsdorf's approach as well. Her own training and experiences left her with the same concerns about potential for future addiction, particularly given the incredibly high doses of morphine, and other drugs Kieran would require. One of the nurses shared her own

---

[13] M. Noel, et al. "Remembering Pain after Surgery: A Longitudinal Examination of the Role of Pain Catastrophizing in Children's and Parents' Recall." *Pain* 156(5) (2019): 800-808.

struggle to shift her belief systems when Dr. Friedrichsdorf first arrived. She talked about how she had to be willing to open up to a new set of literature and a whole new way of thinking. It meant being willing to accept that what she had been taught in her many years of training might not have been the full picture. It meant that she had to unlearn some of her hard-earned knowledge. That took some time to accept and it took more than just understanding the literature.

The nurse opened up to and embraced this new approach once she experienced the impact it had on patients. It became clear how much the approach supported the child and impacted the long-term outcome. She was now deeply committed to this new approach and proud to be a part of helping to shift the dogma by sharing her own learning with patients and clinicians.

In a recent interview Friedrichsdorf, ever humble, says: "At the end of the day, I'd like to leave a footprint in the sand, as we all do, hoping that I can inspire the next generation of young interdisciplinary colleagues to do the right things and to do well in their careers. When I am eventually sitting in Costa Rica, on the beach with a nice drink in my hand, I hope once in a while to get a postcard from somebody for whom I have made a real difference."

> *Dear Dr. Friedrichsdorf, you made a real difference for us. We wouldn't be here without you and certainly not thriving. We hope to not need your clinical services in the future and would love to share a toast on the beach!*
>
> —Erik and Moira

Consider This

Is your current filter supporting what you say you care about? Where is it getting in the way?

In a relationship that's important to you, think about how you can understand their point of view, not just the content they are sharing. What will it take to get curious? What might be in the way?

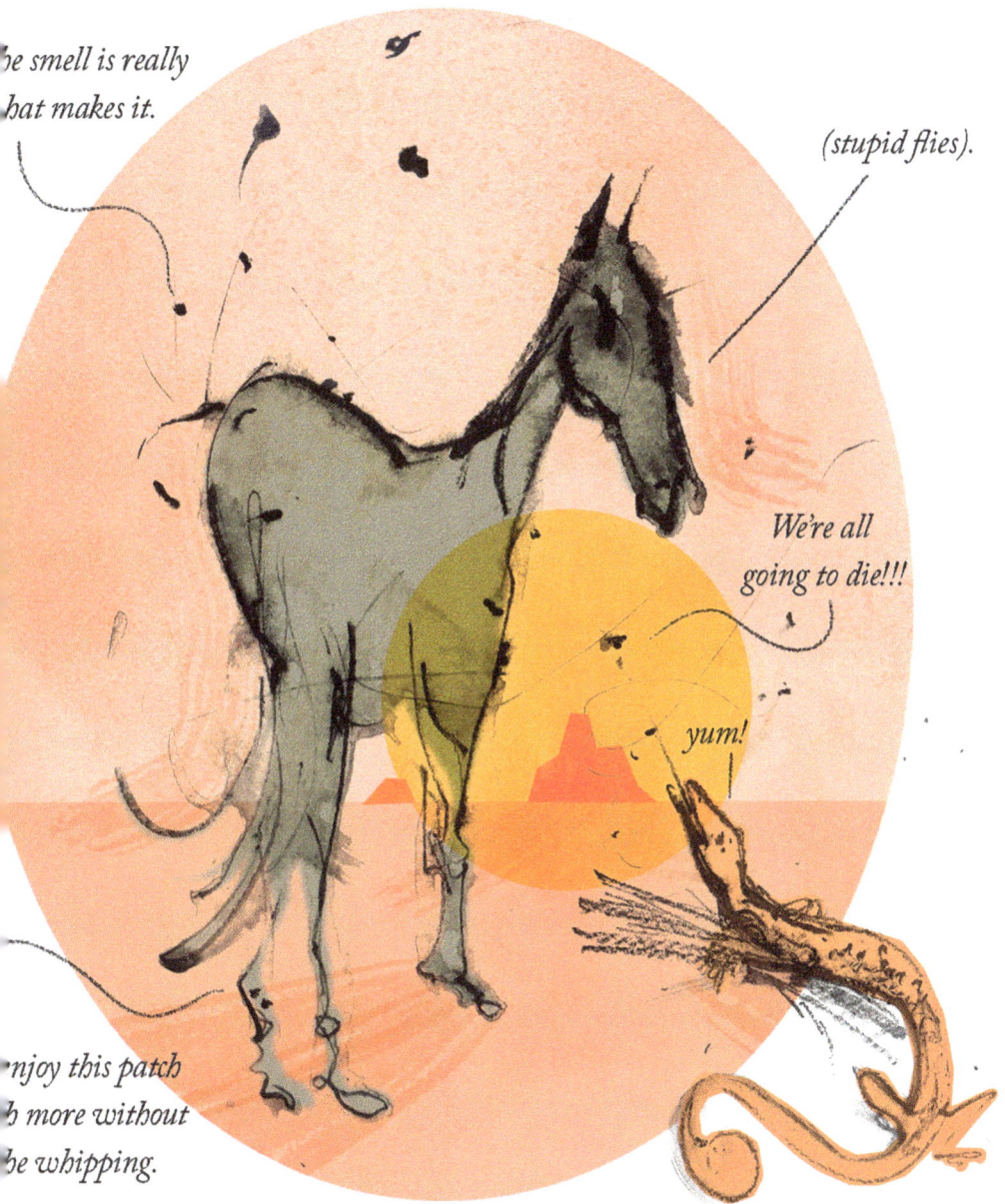

Fig. 5. "Filters" as demonstrated by our subjects and flies.

6

The Stories We Tell

Dr. Fernando Flores was the Minister of Finance in Chile in 1973 when the country was taken over by a coup. As part of the coup, all the cabinet members, including Flores, were imprisoned. Flores spent three years in prison, separated from his wife and children. Years after his release he said:

> *I never told a victim story about my imprisonment. Instead, I told a transformation story—about how prison changed my outlook, about how I saw that communication, truth and trust are at the heart of power.*

Flores realized that the stories you tell yourself and the language you use can limit or open up possibilities for your future. He says:

> *In language we build our own identities, our relationships with others, the countries that we live in, the companies we have and the values that we hold. With language we generate life. Without language we are mostly chimpanzees.[14]*

---

[14] Fernando Flores. *Conversations for Action and Collected Essays: Instilling a Culture of Commitment in Working Relationships*. (North Charleston, South Carolina: CreateSpace Independent Publishing Platform, 2012).

Language creates the stories we tell ourselves and others. It is at the genesis of the actions people take. Some would say that speaking (both internally and externally) is an action in itself. Stories shape belief systems and the filters that impact your view of the world.

After release from prison, Flores would go on to study and write about language distinctions that helped us view our experience with Kieran through a different filter. The distinction between two types of language—assertions and assessments—has been particularly useful in our journey. Understanding these distinctions helped us see how the stories we told ourselves were based on our assessments—how we interpret the world around us.

Erik: Learning From Kieran

When Kieran was young, his intense personality was everywhere. He would bash his head on the floor or the wall when he was upset. At times he would scream so hard when upset that he would stop breathing, turn blue, and pass out. It was scary.

When he was older, he would swear, hit, or find other ways of acting out daily. I had a story in my head about what it meant to parent well. When Kieran acted out in extreme ways, my assessment was that this behavior was intentional, it needed to change, and he should receive a negative consequence. I thought I should put him in his room or give him a time-out.

Anytime I tried to do that, though, things would get worse. Kieran would break or destroy something or punch a hole in the wall. It certainly didn't change his behavior; rather, it made things worse.

Though she struggled with it too, Moira had a different assessment of the situation. She had spent more time with Kieran and realized quickly that my approach wouldn't work. Moira saw his behavior as an appropriate acting out for him, that his history was impacting his emotions. It was the only way he knew how to express how he was feeling.

Moira saw something that required support and love, rather than discipline using consequences. She had learned from his NICU nurse that the best thing we could do was find a way to acknowledge and be with him through his intense emotions—not to try to punish, control or change him.

It took me a while to get aligned with this idea. I had a strong story about what it meant to be a father and society was confirming my assessment, so much so that I felt it was "the truth." Moira struggled with it too. People we respected parented differently and offered advice. Their children seemed well behaved, they didn't scream and swear or throw food and if they did, there would be consequences. That was how we should parent, right?

Moira and I had some heated discussions about this. There were the same set of facts—Kieran acting out—and very different assessments about what that meant. We both wanted to prove who was right, sharing articles and stories that confirmed our individual assessments. There was plenty of grounding for either side.

One day Kieran came home from first grade and asked, "What do I do if I can't live my life?" Our first thought was of great concern for Kieran wondering where this thought was coming from. It turns out, his teacher said that if he didn't get his work done she would tell his parents to not let him ski anymore. She was going to make sure he knew there were consequences to his behavior. In Kieran's mind, he connected those consequences to living his life, not to changing his behavior.

It became apparent that I would need to change how I was as a parent. I would need to focus on how I showed up and impacted Kieran rather than his impact on me.

Both Moira and I needed to shift our assessment that, as parents, we would be doing the teaching. In reality, Kieran was teaching us. Over time, I came to see that my story of parenting was just one interpretation and not *the truth*. Kieran clearly needed a different approach.

I would need to change my story and be willing to show up differently if I was going to support Kieran in the way I wanted, and he needed. We would have to learn to meet him where he was. We needed to enter his world so that we could support him coming into ours.

Assertions and Assessments

Assertions are defined as statements of fact; they can be proven true or false with agreed-upon quantifiable measurement. For example, "it's thirty degrees Fahrenheit outside" is an assertion. We can measure it with an agreed-upon system and prove it true or false. Under this definition, you cannot make an assertion about the future because it hasn't happened yet, so there is no way to measure it.

An assessment, on the other hand, is a statement of opinion that cannot be proven true or false. It is your interpretation and judgement of the data. "It's a beautiful day out" is an assessment. For some, twenty degrees and snowing is a beautiful day to be outside and playing in the snow. For others, it would be miserable.

It seems like a straightforward distinction at first glance.

What you may not realize is that you are making assessments all the time. The amygdala region of the brain is constantly serving to filter out what it deems to be irrelevant information so you can make quick judgements (assessments).

Assessments are really useful and help to keep you safe. They allow you to take quick action when needed. On the other hand, if you are not aware that you are making assessments, they impact your actions without you realizing and without you making an active choice.

While useful in some situations, particularly when it comes to our physical safety (is it safe to go down the alley, is that bus going to run me over, etc.), when it comes to more complex social-emotional scenarios (how should I judge that person who doesn't look like me) assessments can get in the way.

The real challenge comes when someone considers his or her assessment as the truth. Many times people hold their assessments as the only truth.

One person's point of view on whether the day is beautiful or not can become *the truth* or the description of the day, when in actuality that person's current filter of how they see the world is being revealed. They are revealing who they are, their point of view, just as much as they are explaining the day.

Increasing awareness of your assessments (especially when you hold them as assertions or *the truth)* is a tool to help understand yours or another's belief system. It can open up possibilities for a new way of viewing the world.

For us, understanding this distinction, and paying attention to our assessments, helped us navigate the emotional fear and make sense of how those emotions were impacting our decisions. It helped us pay attention to the stories we told ourselves and be open to the idea that there might be a different version of those stories.

Assessments and Decisions

Kieran's diagnosis came with a set of assertions—facts that were quantifiable with agreed-upon tools. His diaphragm on the left side didn't exist, his stomach was in his chest, and his lung-to-head ratio was very low, suggesting a severe hernia.

What came next was all assessments. The first doctor's assessment of the facts was that our child had a 25 percent chance of survival. Although that assessment was grounded in scientific data, it only told us the likelihood of an outcome, not what our child's outcome would be. At first, we took that assessment as the truth. Our doctor certainly had more experience and expertise than we did. What we didn't do is get curious. We didn't ask what was behind that assessment or what the limitations of the data might be.

As we started to explore other options, we realized that there might be different ways of interpreting the same set of facts. When we started to get curious, we were able to ask about the context behind the assessments we were hearing. What did each person care about and what was his or her experience with other babies like ours? Did this person have additional assertions (facts) or experiences to offer?

Ultimately, being curious about what was behind the assessments allowed us to make a decision that felt best for us and our child. It allowed us to find the team that was going to "fight for each individual child." Ours.

The assessments we held and the assessments of the team we chose did not guarantee a specific outcome for Kieran. By changing the story, by understanding what was *truth* and what was interpretation did not guarantee a different outcome. It opened up the opportunity to take an action towards the outcome we cared about. It allowed us to take in information and learn from it, to let us see what else might be possible and not define our world in absolutes.

One assessment closed an opportunity, while another one opened up a different one. Some doors opened while other ones closed. These language distinctions helped us understand which doors were most important to open.

Assessments In Family Business Transition

The second generation of the Anderson family business had taken over from their father when he died about five years previously. Each of the second generation had worked in varying capacities in the family business for most of their adult life. They were grateful for the opportunity that was provided to them by their father and had a desire to pass on "The Golden Goose" to the next generation and beyond. It was very clear that was the founders dream.

Frustration had set in because they were starting to believe they were not going to be able to accomplish their goal. There were no third-generation members of the family working in the business and learning about what had created the long-term success they consistently had.

The third generation was also frustrated. Although they, too, were grateful for grandpa's legacy, they did not feel there was opportunity to be part of the company. They did not believe there was any opportunity in the family business. Most of them had pursued other careers.

The second generation had reached a point where they were considering selling the business. They were convinced there was not enough interest in the business from generation three in order for it to be passed along, fulfilling grandpa's dream.

Each member of the family was feeling stuck. They were close to becoming resigned that there were no future possibilities of continuing with the family legacy to the third generation. Their "Golden Goose" was going to disappear.

When we first met the family members and started to work with them, each generation had strong assessments about the situation and each other.

Pre-Process Assessments Of Two Generations Of The Family	
Pre-Process Generation Two (G2) Assessments	Pre-Process Generation Three (G3) Assessments
G3 is not interested in the family business or in how our assets are distributed.	There's no opportunity for us to add value; G2 "knows it all."
We don't believe G3 will ever be interested in supporting the business or assets.	G2 doesn't communicate and is not transparent about what's going on in business or with our family assets.
G3 does not care about the family business.	We don't know what options are available in the business—G2 won't let us "in."
We have tried everything to get them engaged and create opportunity.	We have given up trying.
G3 is entitled.	G2 is entitled.

This was a family that had a family office and had worked with lawyers, planners, and advisors, all in attempt to keep the family business going and transition the business to the next generation.

Like many families, they cared deeply about each member but were really frustrated with the family dynamics and what they felt was a lack of communication. They had different political and religious views and their assessments about each other and each generation negatively impacted their ability to be successful. These assessments were not revealing a path toward a successful transition. The assessments were creating a future where the founders' legacy would not continue on.

We designed a process to help each generation to start to get curious with each other. We flipped the conversation to allow generation two to start listening to what generation three desired and why. They began to explore what each of them was for, rather than what they were against. What did they desire for themselves, for the family, and for the business? They called it "Family Speed Dating."

After learning more about the distinction between assessments and assertions, and raising their individual and collective awareness, they were able to recognize how their assessments were impacting their relationships. They started to realize that it wasn't about them, but about how they showed up with energy and support for each other. They started to become more curious about one anothers' perspectives and paid attention to their own assessments. Over time, their assessments shifted and they realized that they cared about each other and their future together.

Post-Process Assessments Of Two Generations Of The Family	
Post-Process Generation Two (G2) Assessments	Post-Process Generation Three (G3) Assessments
G3 is engaging and stepping in.	We are grateful for the opportunity to participate. If we are to receive distributions, we want to also add value.
It's amazing how far we have come together in a short time.	We can create a communication plan.
It is clear G3 is grateful for the family business.	We are aligning around what is possible.
We are making good progress toward our new one-hundred-year plan that G3 defined.	We can create a future together.
G3 is stepping up and leaders are emerging.	More and more family members are choosing in. We are seeing our influence and its potential impact.

These new assessments created the opportunity for a very different future. They could start to visualize that future and the impact it would have on each of them. They now began to take collective action to generate that future together.

Generation three began to be more involved in assessing and supporting a new future. They designed a one-hundred-year plan. In addition, the first generation three member joined the family business as a key leadership team member.

They created a vision for the business as well as a commitment to support each other as a family. They designed specific practices for both. Their time is now focused on how to support each other and stewarding "The Golden Goose" together.

Consider This

Take a moment and reflect on what assessments you are holding about others, about the circumstances around you, or even about yourself. How might those assessments be keeping you from achieving what you say you want most? What doors are being opened and which ones are being closed?

Fig 6. Despite some resistance, Horse starts to see a new possibility.

7

Strive For Clarity

Steve Gleason was a star NFL player for eight seasons, retiring in 2008. Shortly after his retirement, he announced he had been diagnosed with ALS which had a drastic impact on his ability to function and possibly contributed to his career ending.

After his diagnosis, Gleason's future was completely uncertain. Each day is different, and he has no idea how much function he will have from one day to the next—only that it will very likely continue to decline. Rather than hold on to some certain outcome or live in resentment, he says:

> I look at human life like an experiment. Every new moment, every new experience, tragic or otherwise, is an opportunity to gain a more accurate perspective and helps lead me to clarity.[15]

When we initially received our son's diagnosis, we found ourselves pushing back and trying to create certainty about our future. We wanted to know what was going to happen before we took action.

---

[15] Team Gleason. Accessed November 11, 2019. https://teamgleason.org/.

When we were faced with the inevitable uncertainty of the diagnosis, there was risk of us seizing up and not moving forward because we didn't know for certain what would happen.

In these moments, whether an uncertain health diagnosis or rapid change in your life or business, we find that a focus on clarity can help navigate the uncertainty. Clarity creates a filter for decision-making to take action even when there are no guarantees about tomorrow.

Erik: Gaining Clarity

Kieran taught me more in the first minute of his life than the rest of my life combined. Not all the learning showed up in that first minute. And, it created context for what came before and what came after.

What did show up in that first minute was just how little control I had. Intellectually I understood the concept of not having control, and that first minute revealed my understanding of what having no control really meant.

My son was being born and not able to breathe on his own. My wife was laying on the operating table with her abdomen open and I had just signed documents a few hours earlier given up all parental decision-making rights to the doctors. They needed to be able to make instantaneous decisions and would not have time to check in with us to consult.

As I was sitting next to the operating table next to Moira, I felt the fear creeping in. I wanted to curl up in a ball. I felt helpless. And then there was a moment of clarity: I had no control over anything around me. The only thing I could control was how I responded to what was happening around me.

As a first-time parent, I believed that my biggest responsibility was to protect this child and create security for him. In that minute I realized all the tough conversations Moira and I had about how we were going to show up for this child were not enough. I was going to need to be that security for my child, and in addition, give this kid tools to operate in an insecure world.

It became apparent that I needed those tools right now myself. There was nothing certain about my child's future or even his first breath. I needed a way to navigate the uncertainty for me and for him.

This realization brought clarity for me. It gave me something to focus on within all the uncertainty. In my role, I couldn't guarantee any outcome for Kieran, but I could make a choice about how I showed up moment by moment.

As I thought more about the difference between certainty and clarity, it became apparent how much I had let fear and a desire for certainty drive my actions in the past. My attempt to create certainty meant my energy went toward what I wanted to avoid—what I was against—rather than focusing on what I was for, what I cared most about.

This distinction opened up a deeper understanding of myself. My desire to create certainty revolved around protecting what I have, what I thought my life should be, what I was good at, and, most of all, protecting me from fear. In this case, fear of not being a good parent. It was apparent there was nothing certain about any outcome I could hope for. If I invested myself in certainty it took me down a path that spiraled downward. I needed a way to open up possibilities, not close them down.

It felt freeing to shift my focus to gaining clarity instead of searching for a certainty that didn't exist. It freed me up to put my energy toward the things I cared most about and to the only thing I could influence right now. I realized that the only thing I could control was my response to the immediate circumstances and how I showed up.

The Challenge with Certainty

Certainty is defined as something that is certain: fixed, settled, indisputable, inevitable, destined, assured in mind or action. In other words, it comes from that part of your brain that wants to keep you safe—to know.

The more certain you were about what was around the corner in prehistoric times, the more likely you were to survive. You needed to make those decisions very quickly without time for conscious processing.

That's an important thing for you to be able to do. To be certain you are right. You need certainty to make quick decisions and take action, particularly when you are in physical danger. And, as always, there's another side.

In his book *On Being Certain: Believing You are Right Even When You're Not*, Robert Burton writes:

> *Certainty itself is an emotional state, not an intellectual one. To create a feeling of certainty, the brain must filter out far more information than it processes. In other words, the more certain you feel, the more likely you are wrong.*

Certainty helps create coherence in the world around you. You rely on it to make decisions, and you can get defensive when your certainty is challenged. When someone has a different opinion or perspective than you, and it goes against your certainty, you can feel threatened. This can be challenging and can put you into a defensive mode.

If you are not aware of this about yourself and are locked into your own certainty, it limits possibility. It becomes a win/lose argument which is not adding value. A valuable skill to build is how you can hold your own certainty, and how it serves you, while being open to another's certainty. By combining the two, together you can make both bigger and more powerful.

Certainty is based on limited information. You can never really know something for sure. Even science is limited in its ability to claim certainty. People like to believe that science is true or false. But there is always some degree of error or judgement, or standards that are "good enough" to move forward. Just pay attention to the rapidly changing science of nutrition—today this is healthy; tomorrow it's not.

Certainty narrows the pathway of choices and decreases your awareness of the inputs that surround you, limiting possibility. Certainty is about keeping you in your comfort zone supporting your competency and capability. It can get in the way of getting to your destination because many times creating certainty ensures you never find the destination you desire.

The Power of Clarity

Clarity is the state of being clear: free from what obstructs or is unneeded.

Clarity leaves room for you to learn and adapt; it creates the opportunity to take action toward a future you want to design. It does not guarantee an outcome; it opens up the opportunity to take an action toward that outcome you desire.

Clarity can be scary. To become clear you often need to expose yourself, what you care about, and what you fear. That exposure creates vulnerability, but it can also lead to a high level of support. With clarity you can take in new information and experiences and digest it rather than quickly filter it out. You no longer have a need to control the information to line up with fitting into your certainty.

Clarity allows new inputs to impact your decisions, create bigger outcomes and increase your ability to learn and adapt and be resilient.

Clarity allows you to be open to your experiences, to see what emerges and learn from them. Clarity leaves room to believe for now rather than beyond-a-doubt thinking.

Clarity is when everything else falls away and you realize what's most important to you. Everything else is noise. Instead of saying you know for certain, you're saying you believe this is the case for now. It leaves room for the possibility that things could shift as new information comes in.

Distinctions Between Certainty And Clarity

Certainty	Clarity
Limits possibilities	Opens possibilities
Trying to control what you can't	Focused on what you can control (yourself)
About being right ("I know…")	About what you are for (what you care about)
Resistant to new information	Open to new information
Comfort zone	Learning zone
Outside world	Inside world
Rigid	Flexible and curious

The more clarity you have the more possibility of finding intersections with others that connect to what each of you cares about. This creates more opportunity and capability to be open to another's certainty. It allows you to get beyond arguing over the issues and instead explore what others care about and why.

Clarity And The Future

Clarity opens up space to make a declaration about the future. Declarations are bigger than a goal, they are a commitment. They live inside us. They inspire the people around us to get on board to help us achieve them. A clear and powerful declaration becomes a roadmap for making decisions, enrolling others to engage and collectively take action to achieve it.

A powerful declaration is rooted in clarity over what you care about and why. Rather than holding on to some certain outcome, it serves as a roadmap for making decisions.

During the days and months after Kieran's diagnosis, we become aligned around how we would show up. At the time, we wouldn't have described it as a declaration. We didn't write it down or hang it on a wall. In hindsight though, through our conversations and our actions, we essentially declared that we wanted to create space for Kieran to determine his life and create what might be possible for him, whatever that meant. We didn't want to get in the way or let our fears, our story or others' stories, experiences, or assessments determine what might be possible for him. We wanted to be thoughtful and stay curious about others' experiences and assessments, but not make them binding.

We would have to learn what that declaration meant in practice and it was often a struggle to act in ways that were aligned with what we thought we wanted to support. The declaration was something we were deeply committed to and became a filter for the decisions we made going forward. When we faced hard choices, in our best moments, we would find a way to come back to what we declared.

That doesn't mean that decisions were easy or straightforward. In practice, it's messy. But they allowed us to take in new information and determine which actions would best support what we had declared.

For example, when we first started taking Kieran skiing, his intense personality and physical challenges meant that he often vacillated between extreme exhaustion and extreme elation. Erik would often end up dragging him off the ski hill as Kieran kicked him in his back with his ski boots because he wanted to keep skiing, or was mad because he kept crashing.

It would have been easy in those moments to give up on skiing with Kieran. We could have created the story that he wasn't ready, his lungs were under-developed, he couldn't handle the cold, it was too risky for him or too much work for us.

We would come back to our commitment and declaration that we wanted to give him an opportunity to create his own experience and not get in the way of that. To us, that meant being willing to come back the next day and try again—to give him the experiences that would allow him to make the choice.

We were scared about whether we were making the "right" choices. At times it was confusing, exhausting and then Kieran would smile and laugh. Those moments of his joy would become our barometer for staying in it with him.

Clarity In Family Wealth Transition

The Bianchi family siblings were in their mid-to-late forties when their father died and left them a significant inheritance. Prior to their father's death, the three siblings had all led successful independent lives and thought of themselves as a close family.

They lived in different cities and made an effort to see each other a couple times a year, enjoying visits with their nieces and nephews and respecting each other's different lifestyle choices.

As the siblings discussed their options, their different perspectives of the world started to come out. They each had very different ideas about what would make for the best use of the money and how to protect it. Their relationship with each other became about the money and their differing opinions about what to do with it.

Their interactions with each other shifted from curiosity about each other's lives to debating the money issues. It became frustrating and disempowering.

Though they were a generous and thoughtful group, their desire to protect their father's legacy had them each suddenly focused on "what's best for me." They started arguing over who was right.

They wanted to be certain of the future.

We were introduced to them through their wealth advisor who was on the front end of helping them navigate this new wealth their father had gifted to them. When their father died, they knew they wanted to protect his legacy. Like many families, their focus was how to protect and not lose any of the wealth their father had worked hard to build up. We collaborated with their advisor to discover what was important to each of them. Collectively we designed an experience for them to create a plan and structure that supported them to steward their relationships as well as their wealth.

When they were each striving for their own certainty, they were focused on controlling the outcome of the money and not losing it. This greatly limited the possibilities. They started judging each other's lives in a way they hadn't before.

Now they were having to make decisions together, so their differences came to the forefront. Instead of getting curious about each other's concerns, they were in protection mode about the money, focused on their fears instead of their desires.

They were wise enough to realize that the money was impacting their relationships with each other in a negative way. Once they were introduced to the distinction between clarity and certainty, they started to shift how they interacted.

Their clarity focused on their collective shared purpose—what they were for, what they cared most about. It revealed their concerns for the future were beyond the money and shifted how they thought about what was possible. Finding their own clarity while becoming curious about each other's allowed them to get out of fear/protection mode and get excited about the possibilities for the impact they could have together.

This shift reoriented them to explore how they could collectively work together and collaborate. It became about the whole. They ended up seeking each other out and supporting each other. Rather than divide the money up, they left it in a collective fund to support each other, future generations and the community.

"This created new possibilities for each of us that we didn't see before," they said. "Our relationships have improved, and we are seeing each other in a whole new way. We are able to let go of the need to know the outcome and focus on what we care most about. We can learn together with the clarity that we all are aligned around supporting our relationships. It has shifted how we interact. We now focus on our concerns and desires, rather than our fears. We couldn't be more excited about the future and the impact we can have collectively."

Through this process they created a shared declaration for their future together. They declared, "We will work together to create the best lives we can for ourselves. United together we will be a force for what is possible." They also created some clear conditions of satisfaction that they believed would be critical to succeeding. They wanted to support each other's passions and ability to pursue entrepreneurial opportunities, along with creating what they called financial synergy that preserved the wealth long term, having the money work for them to create a solid foundation for each of them.

They also believed it was important to invest in people: themselves, their families and others with similar values. This would allow them to focus on their positive impact on the world.

Armed with a declaration the siblings were aligned around, their wealth advisor was able to use it as a filter to assess various strategies and structures for how they could support their desired future, allowing them to make well-informed decisions and take clear actions toward that future together.

Consider This

Where is your certainty getting in the way of what is possible? What could you do to get curious about someone else's certainty and be open to their perspective? Where could you gain clarity to open up to new possibilities?

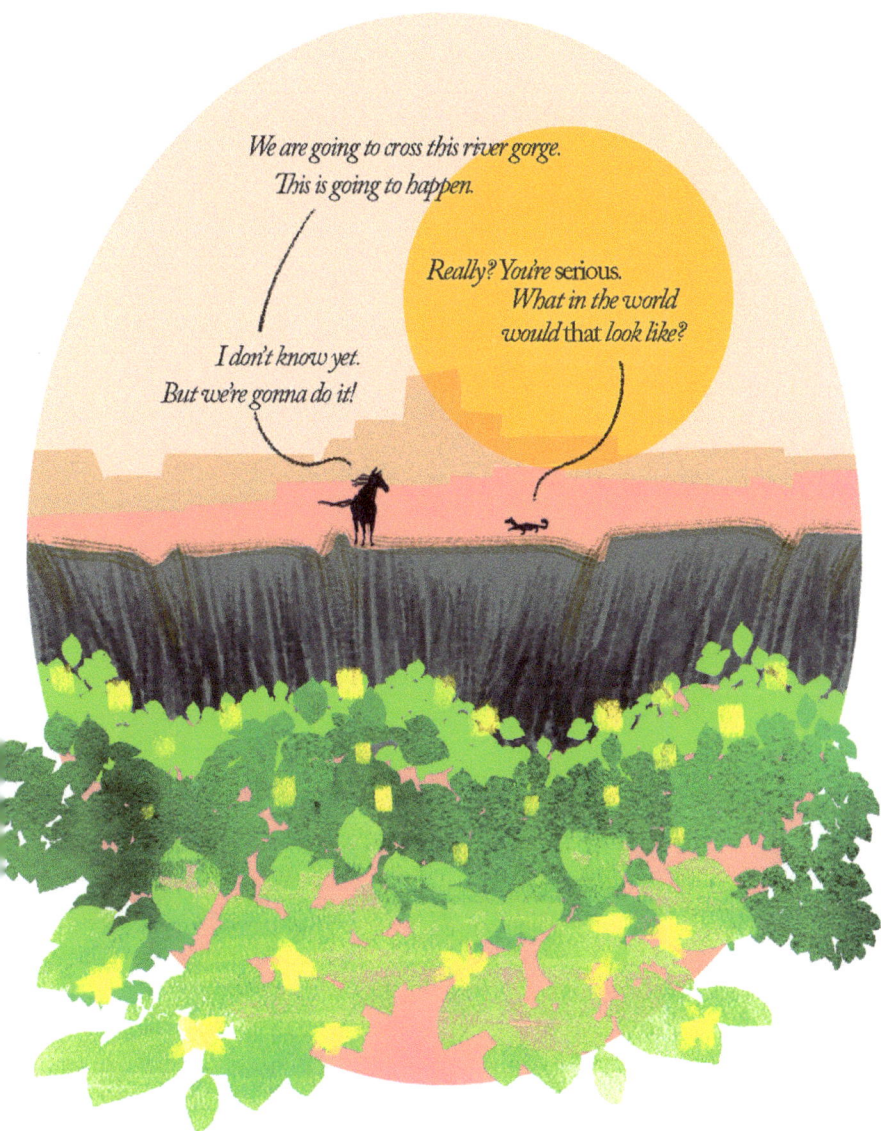

Fig 7. As the sun sets, Horse makes a declaration!

8
The Ordinary Moments

When the sociologist and vulnerability researcher Dr. Brené Brown started studying the concept of joy, she assumed that people would describe unique experiences as the things that brought them joy. What she found was the opposite. She says:

> *Joy comes to us in moments, ordinary ones. We're likely to miss out on them when we're busy chasing the extraordinary.*[16]

She goes on to note that:

> *Joy is the most vulnerable of all human emotions. We are terrified to feel joy. We are so afraid that if we let ourselves feel joy something will come along and rip it away from us and we will get sucker punched by pain and trauma and loss. So, in the midst of great things, we literally dress rehearse tragedy.*

How often do you listen to that voice in your head that's focused on chasing something in the future or rehashing the past? When you do

---

[16] Brené Brown. *Daring Greatly: How the Courage to Be Vulnerable Transforms the Way We Live, Love, Parent, and Lead.* (New York, NY: Penguin Random House, 2012).

it's easy to miss out on the simple joy of the present moment. Often fear can get in the way of experiencing joy.

The idea of being fully present, in this moment, is both incredibly simple and challenging. Your lizard brain (amygdala region) takes over and starts yapping at you, keeping you focused on your fear which will drive your actions whether you are aware of it or not.

The ability to pay attention to and acknowledge that voice, and then let it go and be fully present would be a challenging but critical practice for us as we navigated our experiences with Kieran.

Moira: Finding Joy

When Kieran came home, life was chaotic. There were feeding appointments, respiratory appointments, appointments with educators wanting to make sure his growth and development were appropriate. On many days, he spent most of his time fluctuating between pain and throwing up.

My lizard brain would start yammering at me about what happened yesterday and if he was going to be okay tomorrow. It was so easy to go there and let that worry or fear dictate my actions. It was easy to focus on all the things that weren't working and start to compare Kieran's progress to other kids his age. I could so easily feel miserable and exhausted.

Even on the worst of days, though, Kieran would have at least one moment where he got a huge smile on his face. Moments that I took to mean he was experiencing joy. In those moments, however brief, I felt joy too. This was a new feeling for me—one that I recalled feeling only briefly before. I wondered how, in the midst of all this chaos, he and I could both feel so amazing. I wanted more of it—for Kieran and for me.

I learned to focus on those brief moments and trust that we could cultivate more of it. That was the potential I saw in him. That was the child I wanted to inspire and bring forth—or at the least not get in the way of. The other stuff, even if right now it took up most of our time and energy, I had to acknowledge and find a way to let it go.

Focusing on what I cared about, the moments of joy, helped to push out all the noise and be in our experience. It wasn't helpful for me to focus on what other parents may be worried about or what normal was for a child his age.

It was clear Kieran was on his own path.

Erik and I both continued to find a way to let go of any preconceived ideas we had about what parenting was or who our child might be. We worked to find a way to parent without expectation or judgement and let Kieran be in his own journey.

Getting rid of the noise and being present for our experience helped to redefine what a really satisfying day was for me. Rather than being concerned about typical developmental milestones, I learned to be grateful for a brief smile, a taste of food, even Kieran's tantrums and screaming were something to be grateful for. Grateful that he had a voice and that he could scream. During one of Kieran's surgeries, one of his vocal cords had been damaged, though you would never know it from the volume of his screams. My dad would say, "You should encourage him to scream. It's exercising his vocal cords." A good reminder that there's always another way to tell the story.

This was all more challenging than I could have anticipated. What it meant for me was that I needed to continually practice a way to be fully present in the current moment, without judgement or expectation. It meant not bringing the previous minute into this one and allowing Kieran to be who he was in each moment.

Like our doctors, I learned to assume Kieran would be okay until he wasn't. I found a way to believe in his internal capabilities to adapt and respond.

Before Kieran was born and when he was in the NICU, Erik would talk about the idea that how we showed up would be important to support the best chance for Kieran. I never fully understood what he meant by that. Now, I was starting to realize that *how* I showed up might be the most important thing I could do.

I'd always felt that what I did was how I would create impact in the world. How productive I was, how many manuscripts I published in high quality journals, how much grant funding I could secure. Now I was learning that the energy and presence I brought to each moment, how I showed up, might be the most important thing I could do.

Being present meant living in each moment and finding joy in the simple things. It meant letting go of the past and not worrying about the future. It meant trusting that Kieran would find his way and that my role was to be with him, not to manage him or define his future for him.

Center

The idea of finding center—a place we could come back to and be present to meet Kieran's energy and all that was being thrown at us, with the ability to blend with him, rather than resist—was critical for us. Center was the emotional space where we were present, open and connected. Not judging. Not comparing Kieran's progress to anyone else. Not letting yesterday or tomorrow get in the way.

Center was where clarity showed up for us. It was the space where we could focus on gratitude and find joy in the ordinary moments. It was aspirational, and our fears and the reality of our lives would constantly challenge us and throw us off.

We learned the concept of being centered (as we are using it here) from the practice of aikido, a non-violent Japanese martial art that encourages peaceful resolution of conflict. The concept of center also shows up in other practices of Eastern origin. In aikido, center is a temporary state of alignment of mind, body, emotions, and spirit. It is the place where you are your most powerful and prepared to respond (rather than react) to whatever comes at you.

In a research study of aikido's application to psychotherapy,[17] one participant notes, "In aikido, you have some crazy attacker coming at you, and your goal is to be relaxed and centered and calm and able to absorb and join with, just be there with that energy, in a way that can accept and redirect it."

Another study participant noted, "Learning how to learn is inherent in aikido because the practice is one of going back again and again and again to do the same simple techniques...what is subtle and deep is the quality of the meeting. How present we are, how open we are to change, how open we are to really being there fully."

Richard Strozzi-Heckler, author of *The Leadership Dojo* and founder of the Strozzi Institute, adapted the aikido concept of center to apply directly to the domains of human experience: body, intellect, emotion and spirit.[18]

Center is when you're fully present (body), open (intellect), and connected (emotion), and aligned with a purpose outside yourself (spirit). Until you start to notice what's behind those distinctions it can feel a little esoteric.

---

[17] Patrick Faggianelli and David Lukoff. "Aikido and Psychotherapy: A Study of Psychotherapists who are Aikido Practitioners." *The Journal of Transpersonal Psychology*, Vol 38(2) (2006): 159.

[18] Richard Strozzi-Heckler. *The Leadership Dojo: Build Your Foundation as an Exemplary Leader* (Berkeley, CA: Frog Books, 2007).

Present: To be present simply means to be here right now in this moment, bringing awareness to yourself.

The quickest way to bring yourself into the present is to pay attention to your breath. Notice the quality of your breathing and any physical or emotional tension you might be experiencing.

By expanding awareness of your physical self and of your emotions, you can shift your moods, increase your choices, communicate your own truths in integrity, and listen with greater depth to the concerns of others.

Open: Becoming present in your physical self allows you to open up your nervous system and senses to incoming stimuli in a nonjudgmental way. Opening your senses enables you to be more fully present, providing a depth and texture to your range of experience.

Openness is about awareness of the intellectual chatter. It is about practicing the art of silence and non-judgement. Meditation or mindfulness practices are often aimed at training the intellect.

Connected: When you bring yourself present and open yourself up, you are laying the groundwork for connection to yourself, to others and to your surroundings.

Connection is about emotional acceptance—accepting things as they are and making choices about what to do with those emotions. Acceptance does not mean agreement, just acceptance of what is.

It is easier to find center when things are going well. It's much harder when things are happening that you would rather not be experiencing. Practicing finding center supports the ability to experience those things and take the information in without clouding it with fear or expectation.

As in life, aikido practitioners acknowledge that center is a temporary state. It's not about always being centered. Life will throw you off—constantly. The question is how long do you stay there and how quickly can you get back?

Imagine you are in your fully centered state and ready to respond in a thoughtful way to life's events. Maybe some relatively small event happens and you get frustrated with your colleague or spouse. You move a little off center; maybe you create a little tension in your back or shoulders. You're busy though, so you ignore it. Then something else happens and you get a little more tension in your body and you continue to ignore it and move a little further off center. It may now be affecting your emotional state as well. Pretty soon you're so far off that the smallest trigger happens and suddenly you're at a physical therapist for back pain, wondering why. Or maybe you explode and potentially negatively impact a relationship or outcome that you care about.

On the other hand, if you have a practice of noticing, when you get knocked off the first time, you notice, take a breath and get back to center. You get knocked off again, same thing, take a breath and get back to center. At first, maybe you get knocked off pretty far. It takes practice to notice. Eventually though, you start to notice sooner and return to center quicker.

It's a bit like a surfer on a surfboard, constantly getting hit by the wave and having to find his or her way back to center. Life can feel like the wave, constantly hitting you—and sometimes a big wave knocks you so far off it is hard to get back. You may even fall off. Don't beat yourself up—that takes you further away from center. Just acknowledge it, learn and get back on.

Before Kieran was born and after his diagnosis, one of the doctors told us that we would also have to fight for our marriage. He said that many marriages don't survive something like this. That was useful information to us. It brought more awareness that we would inevitably get knocked off center over and over again. Sometimes so far off it would take us a while to get back aligned.

There were periods of time when neither of us had an intentional centering practice. Even without a specific practice, understanding the concept of center, knowing what it felt like, and just noticing when we were off helped.

Our willingness to give ourselves and each other room to mess up and be willing to find our way back has been a tool that has kept our relationship alive. It helps when we think of it as learning: each time we get knocked off is an opportunity to learn and do it a little better next time. We gain a deeper level of awareness when we're present, open and connected.

Our relationship with Kieran was a mirror that forced us to notice when we weren't centered. He has an amazing ability to knock us way off center quickly and to show us that we're off with his behavior. We realized that often when he was acting out, it was us that needed to change, not him. Over time, we have become better about getting back sooner. Yet, we still get knocked off many times a day. Learning to pay attention and become more aware of our center is a lifelong practice.

For us, the practice of paying attention to our own internal judgements and being open has been particularly useful in both supporting Kieran and our own relationship. Being present, accepting what is, and practicing non-judgement help us to not drag our past into the current moment. This leaves more room for whatever shows up. It helps create space for being grateful for what is and allows us to experience joy in the ordinary moments.

Centering In Practice

Dr. Castile is a highly successful surgeon. He is driven to challenge himself and to positively impact the lives of his patients. Castile also has a passion for downhill mountain bike racing, despite the risk of injury.

When we first engaged with him he was clear that he felt good about where he was as a surgeon, and really wanted help with his bike racing. He told me, "I love this mountain biking and I really want to win a few races. I keep falling just short of the win. Can you help me out?"

We were excited because we found something that was relevant to him, something he had an interest in improving. We felt confident that the work we did with him in racing his bike would also translate into his surgical practice. In our experience, people play games like they play life. Whatever he was doing in his bike racing would very likely be similar to what he was doing in the operating room.

We discovered that before his races, he was thinking of everything that might go wrong in the race and how he was going to avoid it. What you focus on gets bigger. He needed to change his conversation. First, he worked on practicing being centered— to be in the moment, to not be in a future conversation taking away from his ability to execute on his biking.

He developed a practice that started with visualizing himself biking at his best, moving to a centering practice that focused on his breathing so that he could be present in the moment, open to how the race unfolds without expectation, and connected to himself and his bike.

He did this as an intentional daily practice, not just when he was racing. After time, it become embodied in him, so it became natural, a habit.

A few months later he was bursting with excitement and told me, "It was awesome, I won a couple of races. But what I am most surprised about is the shift that happened in the surgery room. The nurses are telling me that they are having more fun and my surgeries are taking less time. I have had more focus, and I feel more confident."

Consider This

Are there times in your life where you feel off center and react rather than respond? What might change if you had a consistent centering practice?

Our colleague Larry likes to say, "I'm going to write a book on managing stress. It is going to have one page and three words. Stop, Notice, Breathe. If you took thirty seconds, three times a day, and did this, in six months, you would be a different person."

Fig 8. Sitting quietly, Horse comes upon a dangerous idea.

9
The Myth Of The Aha!

Ah, the aha! moment:

So inspiring that Oprah Winfrey makes them a regular part of her monthly magazine, shows, and podcast. A Google search for aha! moment returns over 30,800,000 results, including many inspiring stories of lives changed.

Many people look for that epiphany or moment of inspiration that will change everything. Many of our own stories from our experience with Kieran might be considered aha! moments. They are powerful insights that shifted our view of the world.

Ahas can be powerful, at least temporarily. They offer a shift in belief systems so something new becomes possible. As anyone who has tried a quick fix will tell you, transformation does not happen in the moment, but rather over time. The aha! moment itself is not the transformation, but rather the moment that creates an opportunity for transformation to occur. That is when the hard work starts. It is what you do with the aha that determines whether you will create something new.

It takes practice to transform and to take a different action than you've made before. The ability to translate that insight into some new practice determines the level of learning and whether it becomes sustainable. Learning comes when you bring your whole self—intellect, body, and emotion—into it. It comes when you put a new practice in place that, over time, shifts how you show up in the world.

Erik's Aha! Moment

When I was sitting next to Kieran day after day in the NICU, I had many conversations with myself. I kept reflecting on what was important to me. A stressful event of near tragedy can often be the vehicle to gain a sense of what is a priority in life. That was happening for me with this journey Kieran was taking us on.

Day after day I made promises to myself about how I was going to show up when Kieran came home, when he got to the other side and survived these first grueling months. There were all sorts of intentions and commitments I made to myself. I was clear about what type of father I was going to be, what type of husband, and how that impacted who I wanted to be as a person. What was important rose to the top.

Then Kieran came home and reality set in. The life that was on hold for us while Kieran was in the NICU came rushing back. There were bills, work, home maintenance, all the life stuff. I found I put my attention toward those and quickly forgot my newfound energy toward who I was going to be.

I felt overwhelmed, lost and buried, forgetting what was important. I realized I had lost track of what I was grateful for and was focusing more and more on a mindset of surviving each day. My internal story shifted and I started to convince myself that the future was bleak for me and our family.

Eventually, I started to remember the conversation with myself next to Kieran's bed in the hospital. I started to do an intentional daily practice to help me refocus on what was important to me. I began to write down what I was grateful for every day, however small. The practice became the vehicle that reoriented me to what I cared most about. The more I identified with what I was grateful for, the more clear I became about what I cared about and why. It helped me gain clarity on what actions I wanted to take.

My priorities came into focus once again. I could start to better manage the life that rushed back at me. It became easier for me to prioritize and regain momentum for the future.

Six Steps To Build A Sustainable New Practice

Over time your habits support behaving in certain ways, and seeing the world from a particular perspective. This habituation is embodied in our central nervous system—the connections made among your nerves define how you observe, interpret, and respond to the world. These connections are stable; they don't change easily. The good news is that they can change, with practice.

You are always practicing something. The question is, are your practices supporting what you want in your life? If you are not aware of those practices, then they are most likely habits. Habits come out of a practice that is now embodied and automatic. Habits don't develop new neural pathways. Rather, they reinforce the pathways that already exist.

To take advantage of those aha! moments, you need to develop new practices. This requires a willingness to find the time and space to do something different and, as adults, requires not just taking in the new, but also undoing the old. It requires being willing to give up our old way of being, examining beliefs, and letting go of what is no longer serving us.

Robert Emmons, PhD, a leading researcher on gratitude, speaks about the impact of a gratitude practice in his book *The Little Book of Gratitude*:

> *...an increasing awareness that gratitude is vital for individual and collective flourishing is becoming more apparent. Two main factors have driven this trend. First is the mounting evidence demonstrating that gratitude matters. Whether springing from the glad acceptance of another's thoughtfulness, appreciation of the splendor of nature, recognition of the good things in life, or from countless other magical moments, gratitude enhances nearly all spheres of our lives. These effects are sustainable and quantifiable. Second the practice of gratitude is readily accessible, available to everyone. Yet the grateful state of mind, as accessible as it is, can be fleeting, difficult to sustain over the long haul unless practiced with attention and intention.[19]*

Intentional practices are useful to learn something new or increase a current capability. We see six key elements to designing effective practices:

1. Be in choice.

The first step in designing a new practice is to choose to do so. The key is to be aware of whether you are internalizing the commitment to take on changing your behavior. Be aware of whether you are in a "have to" conversation or a "choose to" one. If you feel you have to do it, you are less likely to be successful at sustaining a new practice. Success comes with the internal accountability of committing to and owning it.

---

[19] Robert A. Emmons. *The Little Book of Gratitude: Create a Life of Happiness and Wellbeing by Giving Thanks.* (London: Octopus Books, 2016).

2. Get clear about the capability and/or behavior you want to support.

The clearer you are about the capability or behavior you want to develop, the more valuable and sustainable your newly designed practice will be. Clarity gives you direction and energy. The more specificity you have, the more effective a practice you can design. For example, there is a big difference between saying "I want to have higher sales this month" and "I am going to close five deals."

3. Understand *why* this capability or behavior is important to you.

This is a step that can be easily missed or skipped over. Getting clear on the capability you want is not enough. An additional step is to get clear on the "why." The "why" gets you emotionally invested and intrinsically motivated. It is an investigation into what matters to you and what is behind the desire to achieve the outcome you want. If you do not become clear on the "why," you will rationalize why you are not able to implement your new practice, and you will be right. Your "why" will help you find room to prioritize your new practice. Focus on what you care about, on what you are for, rather than against.

4. Get outside your comfort zone and into the learning zone.

As we discussed, you are constantly fighting your biology to keep you in the comfort zone. A new practice, if you design it correctly, will have you feel incompetent (in fact, at this stage, you are incompetent, and admitting that and tolerating the sensations that go along with it isn't easy). Allow yourself to be a beginner. This discomfort you feel will allow you to learn and grow. Embrace it and don't beat yourself up, knowing that you are on your way to what you care about. Design your practice so that it is not so difficult that you will get discouraged and give up, but also not so easy that you will get bored and complacent.

5. Be intentional and regular.

Effective practices require attention and intention. Now that you have designed your practice, you will want to get the full benefit of the learning it will bring you. This requires that you do it with intention and on a regular basis. Being intentional means that you do it on purpose to support the "why" you are doing it, not just when you notice or are feeling off track. It also means that you do it on a regular basis. Put it into your schedule. Figure out when it fits in with your current routine. It is more important to do the practice for a short period many days a week rather than a large chunk of time once or twice a week. Repetition is essential if you want to shift a behavior and/ or improve a skill.

Human biology comes into play once again. Organisms will always gravitate back towards homeostasis and do what they've always done and find a way to rationalize it. It takes intentional practice and effort for a consistent period of time to change that.

6. Build a community.

Practices are often best done with one or more partners. When you have another person practicing with you, and when you have a commitment to another person to join them in practice, the probability of success escalates dramatically. We have repeatedly observed that individuals in learning communities—groups of people learning together—learn faster and deeper than those who do their practice alone.

Do not expect a change in a week. Behavior change takes time, commitment and repetition. Stay focused on the "why" and the outcome you desire and take small steps to begin with. Once you feel comfortable with this new practice, design a new one to take you to the next level, making sure that you are getting back into (appropriate) discomfort to continually learn.

The Power Of Practice

Police officer Jean Carter's aha! came when she saw the health data from her fellow cops. More than ninety percent thought they were in good or excellent health. In reality, less than ten percent actually were, according to their health screenings.

Carter thought "This is ridiculous. Our officers don't even realize how unhealthy they are. What am I supposed to do with that?" She had been the head of the department's fitness team (Fit-Team) for a few years and realized that what they were doing wasn't working. Something needed to change and fast.

Carter realized that the whole culture needed to shift. The practices people were doing on their own weren't healthy and the health screening showed they didn't realize that. Her vision was that the Fit-Team would support their peers to put healthy practices in place.

Carter explains the challenges ahead:

> *We realized there needed to be a shift but we didn't know what that would look like. I needed to shift the mindset of our Fit-Team to even get them on board. At first, they were there for themselves. They thought "I need to be better at working out for me." As a group, we were really negative and focused on all the barriers. No one believed we could change anything.*

We co-designed an experiential process to help the team see possibilities and put new practices in place for themselves first.

> *During our experiential training, we had this aha! as a team—we realized that we had always just focused on the*

negative, on what we couldn't do, rather than what we could do. By accomplishing the events together, we became aligned around what was possible and our mindset began to shift. We realized we wanted to improve the other officers' fitness and health levels as a whole. It became more about overall fitness and well-being of others rather than just me.

The team left with clarity about what they cared most about and what they could accomplish together. They were energized and excited to implement their ideas.

Their newfound energy was quickly lost, and homeostasis kicked in as they went back to their environment. As Carter explains:

> *We lost it quickly as soon as we got back to the department. You can go for a two-day "rah rah I'm the best," and then you go back onto your shift and it's the same culture. At first, everyone went back to old habits and focused on all the perceived roadblocks.*

> *We had to keep getting reconnected as a team and remind ourselves of why we were doing this. We had to keep choosing in and making that commitment again and again. We used new tools and practiced viewing things through the mindset of "What are the possibilities? Where do we want to get to?" This was something we needed to practice over and over.*

> *We developed an intentional practice to support each other and created reminders to focus on what outcome*

we wanted—on the possibilities rather than the barriers. That's when we started to succeed. That's when we were able to take action towards that outcome we wanted.

Carter talks about the shift in the team mindset that happened over time:

Now all of a sudden on the training days with the Fit-Team I was getting ideas "Let's try this, let's try that..." Instead of knocking ideas down, they were excited and energized again. We started putting together presentations on wellness that people choose in to do. This was a huge shift for a group of officers who don't trust anyone or choose in. These were the things that I thought were cool. We were breaking down barriers to go above and beyond. Then Fit-Team officers started coming in with these ideas and trying new things at their precincts and implementing it themselves. It was amazing.

Consider This

You are always practicing something. Are your current practices supporting what you say you want?

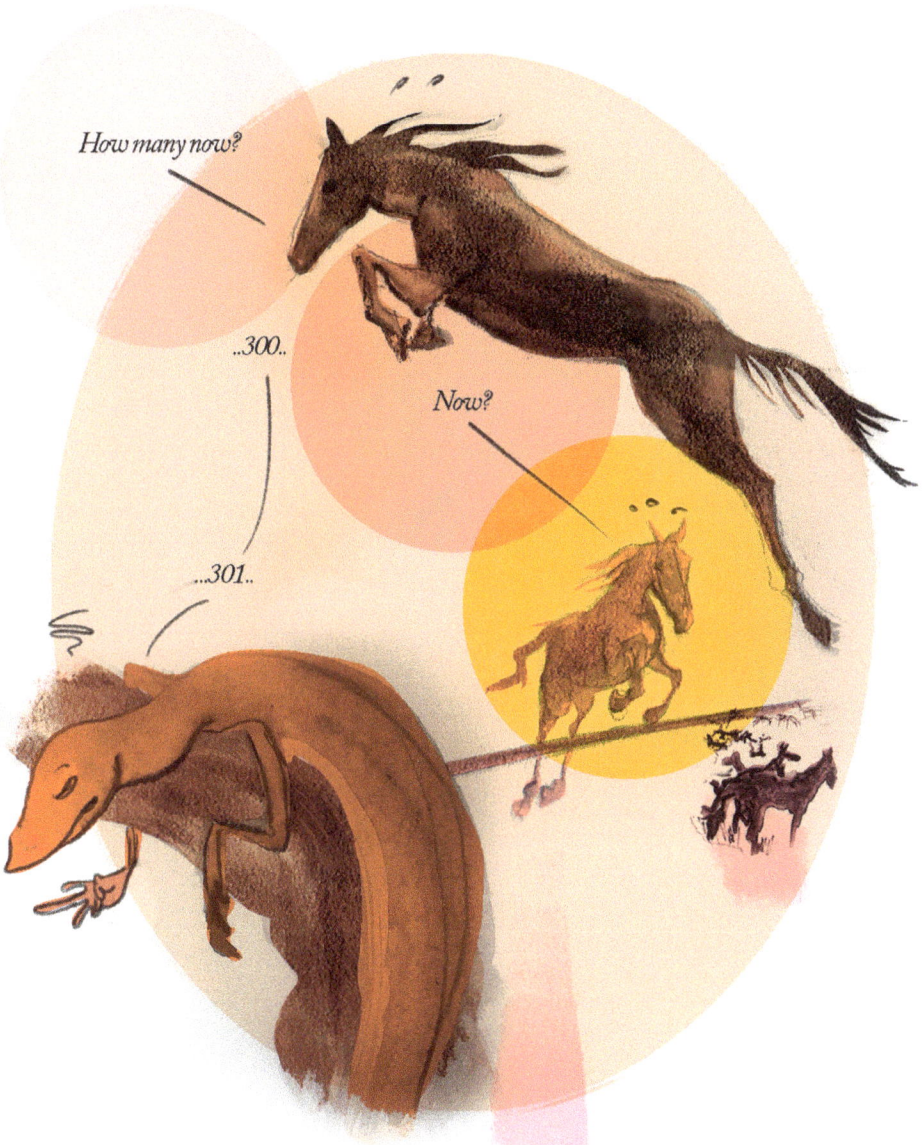

Fig 9. The horse performs the practice ritual under the close scrutiny of a supportive coach.

10
Create A Powerful Learning Community

Humans are pack animals who flourish when connected to other people. They achieve more and become more resilient to the rigors and challenges of life when in a community.

In his bestseller, *Sapiens: A Brief History of Humankind*, Yuval Noah Harari argues that humans survived and thrived because of our ability to come together around a shared belief and collaborate at high levels. He says:

> *Shared beliefs allow us to do the thing that other species cannot. Because we believe, we can cooperate effectively in large groups toward larger aims... Sapiens diverged when we hit on the ability of a collective myth to advance us beyond what we could do individually. As long as we shared some beliefs we could work toward something larger than ourselves—itself a shared fiction.*[20]

---

[20] Yuval N. Harari. *Sapiens: A Brief History of Humankind.* (New York, NY: CollinsHarper, 2015).

The ability to collaborate at high levels is essential for families, teams, organizations, and communities to continue to survive and thrive, particularly in this time of great uncertainty and rapid change. Yet, it can be one of the hardest things to do. Family relationships continue to break down, companies fold, communities break apart, and politics are more divisive than ever.

To collaborate at a high level, people must be willing to fully reveal themselves, be vulnerable, and authentically open up to other perspectives.

Once again, your biology can get in the way. That darn amygdala perceives vulnerability as a threat to your social existence, so it jumps into action and sends out fight or flight signals. You can become anxious and feel vulnerable when you reveal yourself and admit what you don't know. In the book *The Neuroscience of Psychotherapy*, Louis Conzolino argues that, "All anxiety, at its core, is a fear of physical or social death."[21] You react to a social threat, just as you would to a physical threat.

The ability to be aware of your biological response, put practices in place to face that fear, and take action within it is critical to individual and collective success. It starts with one person who is not willing to accept a shallow definition of community and is willing to step into their own discomfort for the benefit of the whole.

In her 2019 Netflix documentary *The Call to Courage*, researcher Brené Brown states:

Vulnerability is the feeling we get when we feel uncertain, at risk or emotionally exposed. There is not a single example of courage that doesn't require uncertainty, risk or emotional

---

exposure...vulnerability is not about winning, it's not about losing, it's having the courage to show up when you can't control the outcome.

Erik: Not Alone

As I spent a couple hours sitting next to Kieran's bed, watching him, I went back to wondering what was he thinking, how does his body know how to fight, how does he already have the will to survive?

I was in a place of questioning myself. How do I measure up, how strong is my will, am I up for the journey ahead, not knowing what that is?

Up until this point, I had achieved what I defined as success at the time, by just forging ahead, making things happen quickly, often doing so on my own and without much awareness of the impact on those around me. It was clear to me this was going to be different. There was so much I didn't know about how to support and care for this child. I would need to find a way to let others in and admit that I didn't know. That felt incredibly scary and vulnerable.

Life can turn in an instant. It continued to be reinforced that I am only in control of how I choose to respond in that moment. I can embrace my vulnerability, or I can try to control those moments and miss out on what life has to offer, the brilliance that is human.

It became apparent to me in that moment life is not about how well I do things, but how well I feel things. The emotions I feel when I accomplish something I care about is clearly what I crave. Those emotions of pride, joy, love, elation, and exhilaration make me feel alive.

I realized that the commitment to an outcome bigger than me is what has allowed me to step into the fear of vulnerability and has generated those feelings on the other side. It was going to take a willingness to be in the discomfort generated by the uncertainty and vulnerability to get to the feelings I craved in the journey with Kieran—the joy and exhilaration.

I realized that I couldn't do this alone, and I needed people around me this time. Moira, the doctors, the palliative care team, nurses, therapists, our families had all made that same level of commitment to support us and Kieran. Without any one of us, he wouldn't survive and certainly wouldn't thrive. It would take everything we all had to support this child.

The commitment of the hospital team drove their desire to study, practice, fail and learn to perform immaculately. Their commitment created the opportunity for our child to be in a position to fight for his life. That is all his body knew how to do on day one, fight for his life, and it was apparent that he was there to play.

The alignment was clear. It was about giving Kieran every chance he could have. None of us could be certain of any specific outcome for him, but we were all aligned around making it possible—or at least not getting in the way of what could be. Even with the experience and expertise each of us brought, we were all learning as we went.

The Power Of A Learning Community

A learning community is a group of people committed to collectively achieving some outcome or solving some problem together. It is implicit that the outcome or problem has not yet been solved and hence they do not currently know how to get there.

High performing learning communities learn from experience and create practices to support what's next. They are willing to take thoughtful action without certainty of the outcome; they learn, refine, and try again.

Typically, in this type of community, someone with the power and authority to do so has made a declaration about the outcomes they want to create, and has been willing to be vulnerable enough to say, "I don't know how to get there," and wise enough to recognize that it will take a new way of thinking and a new set of actions to get there that requires bringing in new perspectives.

The power in a learning community is that each person has a different perspective and brings a unique filter to how each one sees the world. There will be some overlap, but when you bring diverse perspectives together and get curious with each other, you expand what you see as possible. If you're willing to be aware of what's impacting your own filter, and be open to others, you are way ahead of the game.

The concepts presented in previous chapters are largely about raising individual awareness about how you're showing up and impacting opportunities to learn individually and collectively. It starts with each person taking accountability for the whole. Relationships are turbocharged when each individual chooses to be authentic, vulnerable and genuinely care for others. Several key principles facilitate learning communities:

- **Cocreate:** Each individual's perspective is not only valued but approached with curiosity and each person is willing to be open and share views. Sometimes this means you have to "go slow to go fast," as you step back to engage and really listen to each member of the community or team.

- **Filter:** Each member of the community is willing to pay attention to his or her own filter and is open to others. The moment you start to argue about whose filter is right, you lose. Instead, come from a place of curiosity: "Wow, what makes you say that? What are you seeing that I don't see?"

- **Untapped potential:** Each of us has untapped potential. The biggest barriers that get in the way are often your fears and belief systems. In a learning community, awareness of individual and collective beliefs and assessments are constantly explored. Is there grounding for that assessment or belief? Is there an opportunity to see a new perspective? Are you open to a new set of beliefs and possibilities?

- **Experiential:** Experiences expose your filters like a mirror. When you are in only an intellectual practice, it can be easy to fall into your comfort zone and rationalize why things are the way they are. When you are in an experience your behaviors reveal themselves and you cannot hide from them. It becomes information that you may or may not like. It is information that you can then make a choice about and decide whether you would like to make a change.

- **Choice:** Members in a learning community come from a place of choice and pay attention to their use of "choose to" versus "have to" language. Each person takes ownership of their choices and their impact. Individual choices are fully supported by other members of the team.

- **Narrator:** All members acknowledge the constant conversation in their heads and its impact on their behavior and assessments. They are willing to constantly pay attention to their own internal dialogues and "the stories they tell themselves."

- **Comfort zone:** Getting outside the comfort zone in a community turbocharges creating connection and building trust. It creates the opportunity for people to be vulnerable. Courage reveals itself and becomes inspiration for others to take action together.

- **Commitment:** By supporting the community to learn together there is an opportunity to move from a group to a team, which collectively defines a shared set of standards and behaviors that it will take to achieve a shared commitment. These shared commitments become the platform to collaborate together.

High performance shows up when there is synergy among team members, which means the whole has more potential than the sum of its parts. Synergy has two components: alignment and attunement. Alignment is about where you are going, with each person clear about and committed to that outcome. Attunement is about how you are getting there together: practices of empathy, listening, creating trust and creating a dynamic of unconditional support where people care for each other and support individual and collective success.

In our journey with Kieran, our learning community initially included our family and friends and expanded further when we found the right hospital for us. The clinical group invited us to learn with them and made it clear we were part of their team. As much as we clearly needed them, they viewed our perspective as essential information for them to make effective decisions for our baby.

At the time we chose Children's Minnesota as the hospital to care for Kieran, we did not realize their team had just been through a significant learning journey of their own to design new protocols to care for babies with severe CDH. We did not know that Kieran was one of the first babies to receive the new protocol, or how fortunate we were to be there.

A High-Performing Learning Community In The NICU

Doctor Ginny Hustead's drive landed her at the top of her field as a leading neonatologist directing the ECMO program at the tenth largest children's hospital in the United States. She was committed to be better than average. She wanted to make sure every child had the best chance possible. She and her team were committed to continuous improvement and learning.

Her position as head of the ECMO program meant that many of the patients she interacted with were babies with severe CDH like Kieran. "2005 was a tough year," she explained. "It was a year of many difficult patients which added to the commitment to continuously improve our outcomes."

There were ten neonatologists and ten pediatric surgeons that made up the team of physicians caring for babies born with CDH. All of them were highly competent and well respected in their fields. Many of them were well published and well known. However, in 2005, each physician team member had his/her own way of doing things. Their overall outcomes were better than average compared to other hospitals across the country, and they were comfortable with how they were doing things, so why should they change?

Dr. Hustead saw an opportunity to be more than just as good as everyone else. She believed that more children could be saved and have better outcomes. With her desire to learn, and commitment to save more babies, Hustead led an effort to bring the ten surgeons and ten neonatologists together to get aligned around a new protocol.

Her goal was to develop a consistent protocol for the management of CDH babies, from diagnosis (often before birth) to discharge from the hospital, that all the members of the team practiced. She wanted parents, nurses, and other involved medical caregivers all to know what the team believed was the optimal way to treat these complex patients, and follow that approach consistently, and continually evaluate the outcomes. Hustead knew she had a challenge in front of her. "Imagine twenty doctors at the top of their field, highly competent, sharing in the care of these complex patients, and yet each was approaching things differently, based on their prior experience," she explained. "This was not an easy process."

All the doctors had their own ways of doing things that they were comfortable with and that had produced good outcomes in their minds. Why should they even be open to learning a new way? What good would that do when they were already keeping these babies alive as well as almost anyone in the world? If they stepped into new territory, it would just be unknown.

To convince everyone to get on board, Dr. Hustead and her team did the important intellectual work. They gathered data and talked to other hospitals to find out what was working and what wasn't. They analyzed every research paper they could find and looked through their own data over many years.

The real work, though, happened in a different kind of way. Hustead explains, "Before we could get to any alignment around a specific protocol, we had to lock everyone in a room and get connected as human beings. We had to do the hard work to identify and acknowledge each of the individual fears of switching to a new protocol with an unknown outcome.

We also had to get aligned around what we cared about and were committed to attaining together. Once we worked through and acknowledged the individual fears, we found we could all align around the children and giving each baby as much of a chance as possible to survive."

This was hard and uncomfortable work for each individual and for the team as a whole. It took many team meetings to get everything out and eventually agree to a protocol they would all follow. They implemented that new protocol just before Kieran was born.

Prior to implementing the protocol, they had survival rates consistent with the national average of 47 percent for babies with CDH who required ECMO. Five years after the protocol was implemented, they had some of the best outcomes in the world, with nearly 82 percent survival of children who required ECMO.

Their willingness to step into learning changed how they functioned as a team moving forward. They realized that if they wanted to continue to innovate, they had to constantly be willing to get uncomfortable.

Consider This

What have been the most fulfilling teams or communities that you have participated in? What made it that way? What behaviors supported those type of outcomes? What did you do to participate at that level? What could you do even better the next time?

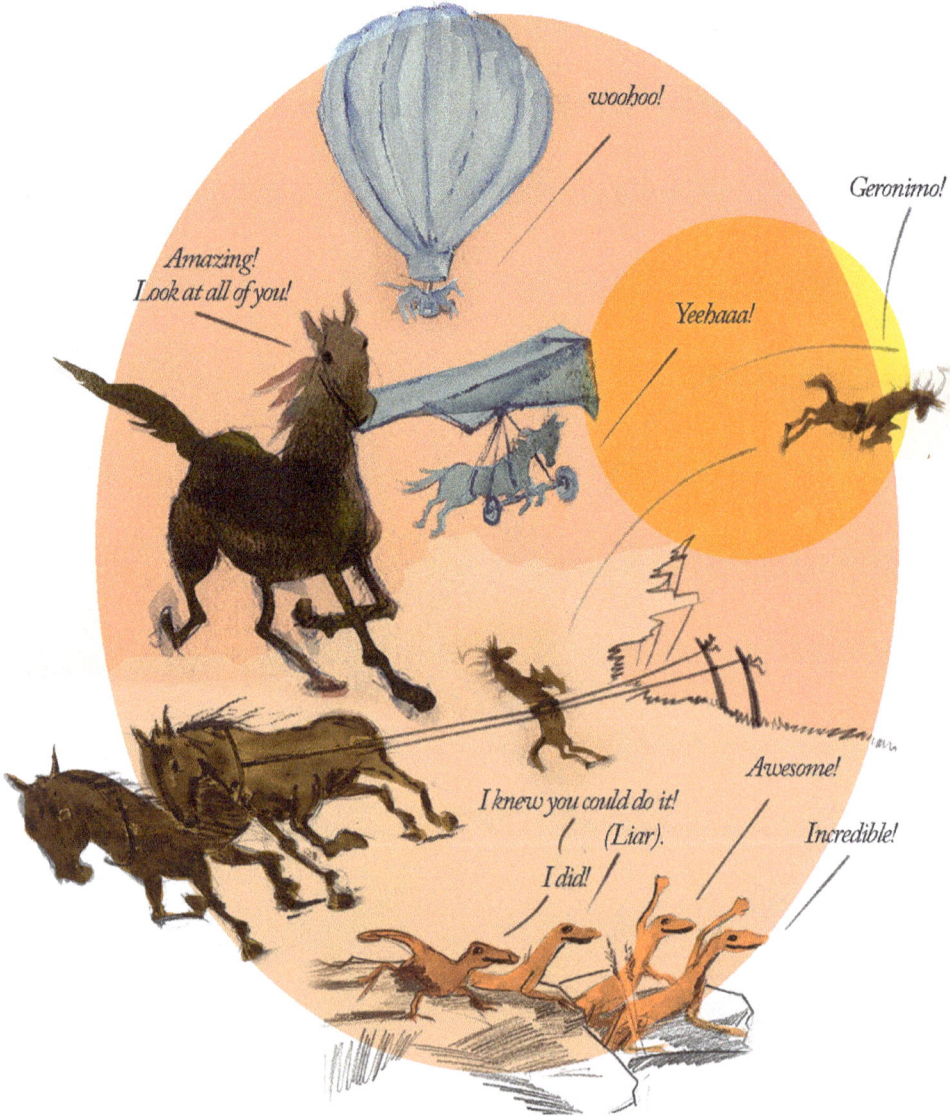

Fig 10. Here we see the inspiring results of a community far outside their comfort zone.

Part Three
Lessons From Kieran

11

Grateful

Erik: Gratitude

Six months after Kieran was born, Larry Burback and I were leading a group on an adventure in the Sacred Valley and the Inca Trail in Peru. We were taking the group to purchase coca leaves to help manage the impact of the high altitude. As we were walking down the street, I received a call from Moira. She was calling me from Minnesota updating me on Kieran's latest appointment with his pulmonologist, just one of the many specialists that Kieran would see regularly.

"He is off of oxygen," she said, before even saying hello.

"What?" I responded.

"We just left the doctor's office and he is doing so well they took him off of it. He is breathing on his own. Can you believe it?" she continued.

I sat down on the curb and cried. I was so joyous and relieved. Post initial survival, this was the next big step for Kieran. I wanted to be there to celebrate with Kieran and Moira—my family. Kieran was now strong enough to breathe on his own. I felt so grateful for the opportunity to be a father, and so much more.

The Road To Thriving

Our new normal meant managing Kieran's feeding tube, doctor appointments, more hospital stays and his intense emotions. Within it all, we tried to make sure Kieran enjoyed as many experiences as possible and tried not to put limits on him. Sometimes we navigated successfully and at other times we failed miserably.

In addition to his NICU experience, Kieran would spend two years with a full-time feeding tube and six months on oxygen. In his first two years, he would have issues with his feeding tube that would require multi-day hospital stays almost monthly, and additional surgeries. He would reherniate and undergo another surgery every year for his first four years of life, making it a total of five diaphragmatic hernia repairs. We would have to navigate severe reflux, watch for scoliosis and asthma, among other things. His emotional life would be understandably turbulent and require our full presence to this day.

Through it all, Kieran has been an incredible demonstration of the power of the human spirit to adapt, survive and thrive.

As of now, Kieran is an energetic, healthy, intelligent, eleven-year-old boy who fully engages in life. He is an avid skier and skateboarder who also loves art, dance and music. His teachers tell us he's a bright, curious and empathetic child. He is constantly playing outside his physical and emotional comfort zone and pushing us out of our own.

Are there challenges? You bet. Kieran is intense, challenging, and never makes it easy or comfortable for us. We constantly worry about his health and well-being—particularly given his history and the activities he's chosen to do. We have to be intentional about finding ways to (re)focus on what we care most about and pay attention to what we are grateful for each moment.

We often get asked questions about how we support Kieran and how he feels about his life. We asked Kieran (K) some of those questions (Q) so he could answer in his own words:

Q: People ask us "How do you let him do these things (ski, skateboard, etc.)? Why don't you protect him more?"

K: How can you not? If you didn't let me ski and skateboard or any of the things I love, then I wouldn't be able to live my life. It's the place where I feel the most free, and I can just let go of everything and my mind is blank. I feel more joy when I'm skiing than anywhere else. You trust I know what I'm ready for and I know what's safe and what's too dangerous to do. And trust is a huge factor of motivation for me. I know that because you trust me, it helps all of us let me do something a little dangerous every once in a while.

Q: Do you worry about your scars?

K: I am proud of my scars. The bad things that happen to me make me who I am. If it weren't for these scars and all that I've been through, I wouldn't be who I am. I know from skiing and skateboarding that I have to crash and get some scars in order to learn and get better. If you don't have any scars, you're probably not risking enough to learn things that are more important than ever imaginable!

Q: Do you feel like you have any limitations in life?

K: Yes but no. At points I know I can't do certain things like certain tricks in skiing. But over the years, with some help, I have realized that if I practice over time, I will eventually have the ability to achieve whatever I am not able or ready to accomplish—yet. Using the term "I can't" is in a sense telling my mind and body that what I am thinking about accomplishing is not a possibility and it will never be possible. But if I tell myself that I will be able to do this someday if I choose to, then that will put my body and my mind in the mindset that will allow me to accomplish what I want.

Q: Do you feel like you have any limitations specifically because of your CDH?

K: At times. Breathing underwater and taking deep breaths I notice it's harder or different than how other people breathe. But I have found ways to work around that and be more successful in life than I was before.

Q: What is the hardest part of your life?

K: Good, bad, sad, emotions. And girls. It's the hardest and the best. Life can be hard, but emotions and girls are the main things I focus on. Other than skiing, of course. Yet all of these things make my life a lot better than what it would be without them.

Q: What has been the best part of your life?

K: Experiencing eleven years of being K-Star (my nickname).

Q: What are the times in your life that you feel fearful? Or where your lizard brain starts yapping at you? What do you do?

K: Well, when I'm skiing, I get nervous about new tricks. I have to decide if it's worth doing right now or not. Sometimes I know I'm ready and sometimes I'm not. Like last year a bunch of the older kids were doing backflips and I really, really wanted to do one. But I knew I wasn't quite ready. So even though they were teasing me, I had to take a breath and trust myself that I wasn't ready yet.

Dad and I made up this thing called "EGG-B, Strong." I use it all the time when I'm skiing or skateboarding or even at school when my friends are driving me crazy. It started because I really like eggs for breakfast, and Dad and I talked about using my magic breathing when

I'm skiing. It stands for: Erase (stop thinking about the last trick or whatever), Go Get it, Breathe (the important part, take a slow deep breath), and Strong (think strong words). I use it a lot and it really helps me in sports and at school.

Q: What's the biggest thing you worry about in your life?

K: That I won't be able to do what I love at any point in my life.

At a follow up appointment, Kieran's pulmonologist told us "I don't think people realize how hard it is to create lung capacity without a working diaphragm. When I see children with severe CDH like Kieran doing sports at that level, I am amazed at what these kids can do, when given an environment where they can adapt and thrive". A powerful reminder to pay attention to when our own fears might get in the way.

We formally celebrate two birthdays for Kieran with family and friends: his day of birth, May 5, and the day he came home from the hospital, July 3. Privately, we celebrate each and every day with him.

12

Let Me Show You My Scars

When Kieran was around five years old a friend of his who was just a few months older was having a critical surgery of her own. When we went to visit her in the hospital, Kieran immediately approached her and sensing that she might be a little sad, he asked, "What's wrong?" His friend said, "I'm worried about having scars from my surgery. What are other people going to think?"

Without hesitation, Kieran lifted up his shirt and said with empathy and pride, "Let me show you *my scars!*"

"Wow!" we thought. It was so natural for him, as a five-year-old, to share himself and connect with empathy. His vulnerability broke down a barrier and put a huge smile on his friend's face.

Later we asked him why he did that, and his response was, "I wanted her to know that she was not the only one."

This journey has left us with many of our own scars, both individually and as a family: scars in our relationships, on our business, and on ourselves. It's been messy and we screw up a lot. We are still learning to embrace our own vulnerability and drop whatever masks we have built up over a lifetime.

So often vulnerability is seen as a weakness. This belief limits the ability to connect to others and build trust. Vulnerability is a powerful connector to not only build trust, but to also inspire others to go beyond their comfort zone, break barriers and reach new possibilities.

Our son has been a mirror that helped us gain clarity about who we are and what we're committed to. He taught us that it starts with our own self-awareness and our willingness to take a look at ourselves every day. He taught us the power of community and what is possible when people come together and commit to something bigger than themselves.

What we know is that life is messy and constantly changing. We learned that the only thing we can control is how we respond to the world around us.

Learning is a lifelong process that takes intentionality and practice to develop behaviors that allow us to be open to reveal our authentic selves to each other and the community around us. Being willing to step into discomfort, making each next choice, challenging our filters to explore our assessments and gain clarity, has allowed us to enjoy more of the ordinary moments, put practices in place and participate in a community that keeps learning.

The risk of not stepping into discomfort and trying to remain safe will keep out what we need most, connection. Connection to ourselves, to the people we care most about, and to the communities we interact with every day. Staying safe limits the opportunities to learn.

Paying attention to our own fears and being willing to step into discomfort has shifted how we parent and how we show up in our lives. Of course, we're nervous every time Kieran goes skiing or skateboarding, when he has a cough or his back hurts, and when he leaves the house for that matter. There is no shortage of things to fear in today's world.

Kieran will need to continue to deal with some unique medical challenges like scoliosis, severe reflux, asthma and diminished lung capacity. Kids with severe CDH often need to eat far more calories as others because daily life takes that much more work for them. So far, Kieran has found a way to navigate through and view these challenges as opportunities to learn and grow. He says he feels strong because of his CDH and all that he's been through.

At the end of the day, our experience and the framework we use are really about recognizing and acknowledging the humanness in us all. There are some things we all struggle with simply because we're human living in the world today. And as humans we are blessed with capabilities to navigate and thrive in a world of constant change and uncertainty, if we are willing to choose to tap into them.

We are so incredibly fortunate to be telling this story. We realize we could be telling a very different one. The principles and framework did not guarantee an outcome. Our experience is that these principles helped create the possibility for the story we are telling. They helped unleash the individual and collective human potential around us moment by moment.

As Abraham Maslow, the psychologist best known for framing the hierarchy of needs once wrote:

> *One can choose to go back toward safety or forward toward growth. Growth must be chosen again and again; fear must be overcome again and again.*[22]

---

[22] Abraham H. Maslow. A "Theory of Human Motivation." Originally published *Psychological Review*, vol 50 (1943): 370-396. Published by the Psychology Classics Initiative.

If we don't pay attention everyday, our own fear creeps in. The fear is always there. It never sleeps.

We keep striving to *let go to fight for what's possible.*

PHOTOS II

At two years old, Kieran looks like any other happy, healthy boy. Though he would have more surgeries to come, you couldn't tell by looking at him how he started life. He loved his strider bike and especially going downhill fast. He started skiing at two and was immediately in love with the sport. He especially liked big jumps and tricks.

We traveled early and often with Kieran even with the hassles and fears about his feeding tube and health. He went on our annual trip to Mexico at seven months, Ireland and Scotland at one and two years, and started an annual trip to the Boundary Waters Canoe Area at four years, among others.

© HoldenPhotos

Kieran feels most joyful and alive when he's outside in nature working with gravity and wind to propel him.

Photo Credit: Eric Barron

Acknowledgements

We owe much gratitude to Henry DeVries, our editor/publisher, and the team at Indie Books International, without whom our book would surely still be living in the cobwebs of our minds.

There's a much bigger story than we were able to fully share in this book about the team at Children's Minnesota and the work they do every day. We recently toured the new perinatal center and pain clinic and were deeply inspired by the many hardworking people who sacrifice their personal lives to strive for better outcomes and care for families like ours daily. They are breaking belief barriers, working outside their comfort zones and saving lives each and every day. Anything we say feels inadequate to fully express our gratitude to the doctors, nurses, administrators and donors who support this amazing team.

Several of the clinicians who cared for Kieran before and after birth took time from their very busy schedules to share their stories with Erik and provided inspiration and encouragement for this book: Dr. David Schmeling, Kieran's rockstar surgeon who we were fortunate to have perform all five of his diaphragmatic hernia surgeries; Dr. Roy Maynard, Kieran's pulmonologist who was a key sounding board for us in the NICU and in the years after; Dr. Ginny Hustead who directed the team in those first critical hours and days after Kieran's birth; Dr. Ron Hoekstra, one of the key NICU doctors; and

Dr. Stefan Friedrichsdorf, pioneer of the pain clinic. We are so grateful for your clinical time, energy and the insights and stories you each shared.

The other part of the story we weren't able to adequately tell in this book was the deep and fully committed support we had from our families, especially Moira's "mum" Libby, our sister-in-law Maggie, and Grandpa Pat, all of whom supported us and Kieran unconditionally and without expectation. They all stepped into their own learning zones and showed up anytime we asked, and even when we didn't. Of course, it's hard to name just a few because there were so many others who did the same—including Kieran's cousins who lovingly endured the intensity of his emotions, his uncles Colin and Martin and Erik's family, Chris, Gary and Jason. We wouldn't be here without you.

There are many friends, mentors, colleagues and clients we have been so incredibly fortunate to work with who supported us in the years before, during, and after, and who have inspired us in countless ways through their own stories and vulnerability. Each of you contributed to the perspective we have today. Thank you for sharing your whole selves. What a gift.

We are so grateful to our mentor, colleague and friend, Larry Burback, who took a chance on Erik many years ago and created the opportunity for both of us to be in the human potential work we now practice. Larry taught us both to be more patient and aware of our own stories and stayed with us through the struggles and messiness of navigating our business and lives.

Many people provided comments and insights that helped us sort through how to share this story and inspired us to keep going. Thank you to: Our good friends clinician Dr. Peter Melchert, Chris and Josh, for making the hours on the chairlift so engaging and fun; Grandpa Pat, our taxi service and dispenser of grandpa wisdom "you can have anything you want, but not everything you want"; Ron Lenz, for your vision of creating community; Avi Kantor for your powerful collaboration and sharing the local lines at Jackson Hole with us; and Lisa Davis and Jean Schwalen, for your honesty, friendship and laughter.

Paul and Melinda Batz and the team at Good Leadership Enterprises, you inspired us to share our story and realize that both our voices were needed. Thank you for giving us a platform to test and learn.

LeAne Rutherford who put up with Erik trying to write this story in the early phases and supported him to learn what it would take to get his thoughts down in words others could understand. Your encouragement and coaching made this book possible.

Dr. Nancy Knop, our dear friend, mentor, and colleague who passed away during our writing of this book provided invaluable insight, understanding and empathy. You are deeply missed.

To the many people who collaborated and pioneered the human potential work along with Larry including: Chris Majer, Dr. Richard Strozzi-Heckler, Scott Coady and Richard McDonald. Thank you for putting your innovative work out into the world.

Finally, to our friends and family who shared meals, trail runs, backcountry adventures, bike rides, wine, beer and laughter. You helped us stay sane during our journey. We are so grateful to have each of you in our lives.

About The Authors

Erik Gabrielson and Moira Petit cofounded Activ8 in 2010 to support healthy high performing communities. They believe that untapped potential lives in us all, and often it is current limiting beliefs and fears that get in the way of what is possible. Together they bring a rich mix of knowledge and experience that support coaching, connecting, and engaging families, teams and communities. Their experience with their unborn son's diagnosis brought those tools alive in their own lives, which they now speak and write about.

For the past eighteen years, Erik has focused on coaching individuals, families, and teams to see and commit to reaching new levels of individual and collective potential. He grew up alpine ski racing where he learned the value of taking action within fear and experiencing the exhilaration that waits on the other side. Erik has leveraged his experience to help teams and multigenerational families unleash the power of their people in business and family relationships.

Moira spent the early part of her career in academia teaching and researching high performing athletes and applying that learning into a focus of building healthy active communities across various populations with limited resources. Her published, peer-reviewed research articles and book chapters on issues related to sports medicine, physical activity, and health became a launch pad to apply her research into supporting clients as they strive for new levels of health and performance.

Erik and Moira live with their son and Labrador in Saint Paul, Minnesota where they enjoy being outside in all four seasons.

Find out more about the authors and their work at:
https://www.activ8-u.com/

Additional Resources

Additional stories, case studies, resources and downloads are available at: https://www.ourfearneversleeps.com

Works Referenced

Adolphs, Ralph. "The Biology of Fear." *Current Biology*. 23(2) (2013): R79–R93. Cell Press.

Bateson, Gregory. "The Logical Categories of Learning and Communication." From *Steps to an Ecology of Mind* (University of Chicago Press, 1972, 2000).

Brown, Brené. *Daring Greatly: How the Courage to Be Vulnerable Transforms the Way We Live, Love, Parent, and Lead*. (New York, NY: Penguin Random House, 2012).

Brown, Brené. *Rising Strong: The Reckoning. The Rumble. The Revolution*. (New York, NY: Simon Walker, 2015).

Bryant, John. *3:59.4. The Quest to Break the 4-minute Mile*. (New York, NY: Penguin Random House, 2005).

Burton, Robert A. *On Being Certain: Believing You Are Right Even When You're Not*. (New York, NY: St. Martin's Press, 2008).

Conzolino, Louis. *The Neuroscience of Psychotherapy: Healing the Social Brain*, 2nd ed. (New York, NY: WW Norton & Company, 2010).

Emmons, Robert A. *The Little Book of Gratitude: Create a Life of Happiness and Wellbeing by Giving Thanks.* (London: Octopus Books, 2016).

Flores, Fernando. *Conversations for Action and Collected Essays: Instilling a Culture of Commitment in Working Relationships.* (North Charleston, South Carolina: CreateSpace Independent Publishing Platform, 2012).

Frankl, Victor E. *Man's Search for Meaning: An Introduction to Logotherapy.* (New York, NY: Simon & Schuster, 1946).

Faggianelli, Patrick and David Lukoff. "Aikido and Psychotherapy: A Study of Psychotherapists who are Aikido Practitioners." *The Journal of Transpersonal Psychology*, Vol 38(2) (2006): 159.

Harari, Yuval N. *Sapiens: A Brief History of Humankind.* (New York, NY: CollinsHarper, 2015).

Heathcote, Lauren. "On a Mission to Eradicate Pain and Suffering: A Promise for Better Pediatric Pain Care—A Conversation with Stefan Friedrichsdorf." International Association for the Study of Pain (IASP) Pain Research Forum (August 27, 2018).

Maslow, Abraham H. "A Theory of Human Motivation." Originally published *Psychological Review*, vol 50 (1943): 370-396. Published by the Psychology Classics Initiative.

"New Measure of Human Brain Processing Speed." *MIT Technology Review.* August 25, 2009. Accessed on November 11, 2019 https://www.technologyreview.com/s/415041/new-measure-of-human-brain-processing-speed/.

Noel, M., JA Rabbitts, GG Tai, TM Palermo. "Remembering Pain after Surgery: A Longitudinal Examination of the Role of Pain Catastrophizing in Children's and Parents' Recall." *Pain* 156(5) (2019): 800-808.

Peetsold, M.G., HA Heij, CM Kneepkens, AF Nagelkerke, J Huisman, RJ Gemke. "The long-term follow-up of patients with a congenital diaphragmatic hernia: a broad spectrum of morbidity." *Pediatric Surgery International* 25 (2009):1-17.

Savage, Roz. *Stop Drifting, Start Rowing.* (New York, NY: Hay House, 2013).

Strozzi-Heckler, Richard. *The Leadership Dojo: Build Your Foundation as an Exemplary Leader* (Berkeley, CA: Frog Books, 2007).

Team Gleason. Retrieved from: https://teamgleason.org/

Wheatly, Margaret J. "Innovation Means Relying on Everyone's Creativity: Leader to Leader," Spring 2001. Accessed November 11, 2019   https://www.margaretwheatley.com/articles/innovationmeans. html.

Wind, Yoram (Jerry) and Colin Crook. *The Power of Impossible Thinking: Transform the Business of Your Life and the Life of Your Business* (Upper Saddle River, New Jersey: Prentice Hall, 2006).

www.ingramcontent.com/pod-product-compliance
Lightning Source LLC
Chambersburg PA
CBHW040924210326
41597CB00030B/5164